External Research Associates Program

RESOLVING INSURGENCIES

Thomas R. Mockaitis

June 2011

This manuscript was funded by the U.S. Army War College External Research Associates Program. Information on this program is available on our website, *www.StrategicStudiesInstitute. army.mil*, at the Opportunities tab.

*****

FOREWORD

Counterinsurgency remains the most challenging form of conflict conventional forces face. Embroiled in the longest period of sustained operations in its history, the U.S. Army maintains a fragile peace in Iraq and faces a chronic insurgency in Afghanistan. In much of Africa, Asia, and Latin America, active insurgent conflicts continue and potential ones abound. The United States may become involved in some of these conflicts, either directly or by providing aid to threatened governments. Understanding how insurgencies may be brought to a successful conclusion is, therefore, vital to military strategists and policymakers.

The author, Dr. Thomas Mockaitis, examines in great detail how past insurgencies have ended and how current ones may be resolved. Drawing upon a dozen cases over half a century, the author identifies four ways in which insurgencies have ended. Clearcut victories for either the government or the insurgents occurred during the era of decolonization, but they seldom happen today. Recent insurgencies have often degenerated into criminal organizations committed to making money rather than fighting a revolution, or into terrorist groups capable of nothing more than sporadic violence. In a few cases, the threatened government has resolved the conflict by co-opting the insurgents. After achieving a strategic stalemate and persuading the belligerents that they have nothing to gain from continued fighting, these governments have drawn the insurgents into the legitimate political process through reform and concessions. This monograph concludes that such a co-option strategy offers the best hope of success in Afghanistan and in future counterinsurgency campaigns.

DOUGLAS C. LOVELACE, JR.
Director
Strategic Studies Institute

ABOUT THE AUTHOR

THOMAS R. MOCKAITIS is Professor of History at DePaul University. He team-teaches terrorism and counterterrorism courses internationally with other experts through the Center for Civil-Military Relations at the Naval Post-Graduate School. He was the 2004 Eisenhower Chair at the Royal Military Academy of the Netherlands. He has also lectured at the NATO School, the U.S. Marine Corps Command and Staff College, and the Canadian Forces Staff College, and presented papers at the Pearson Peacekeeping Center (Canada), the Royal Military Academy Sandhurst (UK), and the Austrian National Defense Academy. A frequent media commentator on terrorism and security matters, Dr. Mockaitis has provided commentary on Public Television, National Public Radio, BBC World News, all major Chicago TV stations, and various local radio programs. He appears regularly as a terrorism expert for WGN-TV News. He is the 2008 recipient of the DePaul Liberal Arts and Sciences Cortelyou-Lowery Award for Excellence in Teaching, Scholarship, and Service. Dr. Mockaitis is the author of *Iraq and the Challenge of Counterinsurgency* (Westport, CT: Praeger, 2008), *The "New" Terrorism: Myths and Reality* (Westport, CT: Praeger, 2007), *The Iraq War: Learning from the Past, Adapting to the Present, and Preparing for the Future* (Carlisle, PA: Strategic Studies Institute, U.S. Army War College, 2007), *Peacekeeping and Intrastate Conflict: the Sword or the Olive Branch?* (Westport, CT: Praeger, 1999), *British Counterinsurgency in the Post-Imperial Era* (Manchester, UK: University of Manchester Press, 1995), and *British Counterinsurgency: 1919-1960* (London, UK: Macmillan, 1990).

He co-edited *Grand Strategy and the War on Terrorism* with Paul Rich, (London, UK: Frank Cass, 2003) and *The Future of Peace Operations: Old Challenges for a New Century* with Erwin Schmidl (a special issue of *Small Wars and Insurgencies*, London, UK: Taylor and Francis 2004). He is an editor of *Small Wars and Insurgencies* and has also published numerous articles on unconventional conflict. His most recent book, a biography of Osama bin Laden, was published by Greenwood in early 2010. Dr. Mockaitis earned his B.A. in European history from Allegheny College, and his M.A. and Ph.D. in modern British and Irish history from the University of Wisconsin-Madison.

SUMMARY

The study of counterinsurgency (COIN) has focused disproportionately on its operational and tactical aspects at the expense of larger strategic considerations. Foremost among these neglected considerations is the vexing problem of how insurgencies actually end. Most studies presume that insurgencies, like conventional wars, conclude with a clear-cut victory by one side or the other. Preoccupation with the anti-colonial insurgencies following World War II has reinforced this thinking. However, consideration of a broader selection of conflicts reveals that most did not end in such a clear, decisive manner.

This monograph examines 12 insurgencies clustered in four groups based upon how they ended: conflicts in which the insurgents won; conflicts in which the government won; insurgencies that degenerated into mere terrorism or criminality; and insurgencies resolved by co-opting the insurgents into legitimate politics through a negotiated settlement and reintegrating them into normal social life. The author argues that Group 4 insurgencies provide the best examples from which to derive lessons relevant to the United States acting in support of a state threatened with insurgency. From these lessons, a political strategy of co-option can be developed—a strategy combing diplomatic, informational, military, economic, financial, intelligence, and law enforcement assets in a unified effort. However, such a strategy can only work when there is sufficient political will to sustain the protracted effort necessary for it to succeed.

The monograph concludes with consideration of the wars in Iraq and Afghanistan. Based on conclusions derived from the 12 case studies, it argues that the United States has devised the correct strategy for resolving the Iraq War, and that sufficient political will exists to see the conflict through to a successful conclusion. The prognosis for Afghanistan is far less optimistic. The United States adopted the correct strategy for that war only in 2009, long after the conflict had become a chronic insurgency in which the Taliban fund their operations through the opium trade and exercise shadow governance over much of the country. The conflict has also spread to Pakistan, which has proven to be a most reluctant ally. Under these circumstances, the chances of a clear-cut victory are remote. Even achieving a compromise peace through co-option will be difficult. The United States must consider that it might have to withdraw without a satisfactory resolution to the insurgency. In that case, it will need to engage whoever governs Afghanistan to hold them accountable for terrorism launched from Afghan territory.

RESOLVING INSURGENCIES

INTRODUCTION

Upon assuming command of U.S. forces in Afghanistan, General David Petraeus announced to his troops that "we are in this to win." Any commander taking over after the removal of his predecessor amid a storm of controversy and growing concern about a timetable for withdrawal would, of course, be expected to make such an assertion. However, the general's remarks raise a nagging question that has plagued operations in both Iraq and Afghanistan. What exactly does winning a contemporary counterinsurgency (COIN) campaign mean—destruction of the insurgent organization, elimination of insurgent leaders, creation of a peaceful stable state that can defend itself, or some kind of negotiated settlement? Difficulty answering this question stems from a disconnect between military and political strategy.

U.S. Military doctrine focuses on the use or threat of force to support a COIN campaign. It also calls for America's armed forces to lend their considerable assets (transport, logistics, medical, etc.) to the nonkinetic aspects of the campaign. Based upon this doctrine, the Pentagon devises a strategy for bringing its assets to bear on the insurgents. However, since kinetic operations form but one part of a comprehensive COIN strategy, neither military doctrine nor the planning that flows from it can (nor should) devise such a strategy, which must come from the political leadership. Unfortunately, that leadership frequently relies on the military to solve political problems: "In case of emergency dial, 1-800 CALL ARMY." As one commentary incisively put it, "There is a studied lack of acknowledgement on the part of the U.S. Government that the Long War cannot be fought via conventional warfare or through a superficial recasting of insurgency and counterinsurgency."[1] Even when they do recognize the need for economic and political reforms, policymakers often subordinate these efforts to the military effort.

While the situation has improved over the past 3 years with the adoption of new approaches to the conflicts in Iraq and Afghanistan, the challenge of devising a comprehensive COIN strategy remains. Nowhere is this challenge more clearly articulated than in the *U.S. Government Counterinsurgency Guide*. Produced under the direction of the Military Affairs Bureau of the State Department in 2009, this interagency publication identifies the three components of an effective COIN campaign: security, economic development, and information operations. These three components, it insists, should be integrated through a political strategy "providing a framework of political reconciliation, genuine reform, popular mobilization, and governmental capacity-building around which all other programs and activities are organized." The ultimate goal of this comprehensive strategy is "to enable the affected government to control its environment, such that the population will, in the long run, support it rather than the insurgents."[2] However, it is precisely the formulation of this integrative political strategy that is so often missing from U.S. COIN campaigns. More often than not, the government deploys the military in hopes of producing a purely kinetic solution to a complex political problem and only belatedly develops a comprehensive plan for employing other elements of national power. Even then, economic and political strategies often operate independently of or only loosely connected to the military effort. Such was the case for the first few years of the COIN campaigns in both Afghanistan and Iraq.

Failure to devise a political strategy before beginning a campaign may owe something to how COIN has been studied. Despite repeated lip-service paid in so many analyses to winning hearts and minds and to the primacy of politics, researchers have concentrated disproportionately on the military dimension of COIN, focusing in particular on operational and tactical matters at the expense of larger strategic considerations. Foremost among these neglected considerations is the vexing problem of how precisely insurgencies end. Many academics, and more policymakers, appear to operate on the assumption that victory consists in defeating the insurgents by killing or capturing their leaders and destroying their organizations. This limited notion of end-state arises from the selection of COIN campaigns upon which many military and academic researchers have usually focused. In his 2006 article on subversion, William Rosenau commented on the concerted effort to mine historical examples for answers to contemporary problems. "Scholars and practitioners have recently reexamined 19th- and 20th-century COIN campaigns waged by the United States and the European colonial powers," he observed, "much as their predecessors during the Kennedy administration mined the past relentlessly in the hope of uncovering the secrets of revolutionary guerrilla warfare."[3] The problem with much of this research, however, is that while some past campaigns are sufficiently analogous to contemporary conflicts to provide useful lessons, others are not. David Kilcullen sounded a note of caution about the enthusiasm with which analysts embrace the "'proven' COIN methods" of classical COIN campaigns. "Today's insurgencies differ significantly—at the level of policy, strategy, operational art, and tactical technique—from those of earlier eras," he concluded.[4] Preoccupation with the anti-colonial insurgencies following World War II in particular has reinforced the notion that the destruction of the insurgent organization is the best and most feasible outcome for a COIN campaign.

A new and growing body of literature has moved beyond study of the classic insurgencies, but a great deal more work remains to be done. Ben Connable and Martin C. Libicki, in *How Insurgencies End*, offer a detailed quantitative analysis of over 70 cases based upon outcome considered within the context of variables such as control of territory and outside support.[5] However, the sheer number of cases precludes detailed analysis of any of them, and some such as the Bosnia war were not even insurgencies. Still the work provides a very useful macro view of insurgent trends and patterns to inform more focused studies, and it does offer very good conclusions. *Victory has a Thousand Fathers* by Christopher Paul, Colin P. Clarke, and Beth Grill exams 20 different approaches to COIN based on 57 variables applied to 30 cases divided into two categories, wins and losses for the government. It divides campaigns into phases, each of which it considers based upon 19 factors. The study concludes by identifying best COIN practices.[6] It also examines conflicts such as Bosnia that are not insurgencies, and it employs a very complex quantitative model. However, it too contains a wealth of good information leading to an incisive conclusion identifying good approaches to COIN.

This monograph builds upon these and other recent works but takes a different approach.[7] It examines only 12 cases in order to focus on each in greater depth and explores a single variable, how the conflicts were ultimately brought to a conclusion. It argues that those cases resolved by a strategy of co-option are most relevant today and concludes with recommendations on how to develop such a strategy and its implications for the current wars in Iraq and Afghanistan.

APPROACH

This monograph examines past insurgencies grouped into four broad categories based on their outcome: cases in which the insurgents won a clear-cut victory, cases in which the government decisively defeated the insurgents, cases in which the insurgency degenerated into mere terrorism or criminality, and cases in which the government resolved the conflict by co-opting the insurgents. It focuses on the last category, whose examples bear the closest resemblance to the current conflicts in Iraq and Afghanistan and probably to future insurgencies as well.

Cases were selected based upon factors that heighten their relevance as examples in each category. The most important factor is the presence of an outside power in all 12 of them. In each case, the threatened government was either an occupying nation trying to set up and support an indigenous government, or a foreign power intervening to aid an ally threatened by insurgency. The United States currently offers COIN support to two threatened governments, and it will undoubtedly come to the aid of threatened states in the future. The campaigns span just shy of 60 years, beginning with the Zionist insurgency against British rule in Palestine (1945-47) and ending with the conflict in Sierra Leone (1991-2002). While earlier campaigns still offer valuable tactical and operational lessons, they occurred under circumstances sufficiently different from those of today as to render their value as strategic examples highly questionable. The cases in this monograph also include insurgencies motivated by diverse ideologies (secular nationalism, Marxism, ethnocentrism, and religious nationalism). While all insurgencies arise from popular dissatisfaction with social and economic conditions, the ideology that harnesses this discontent varies with time and place. No ideology seems to offer any particular advantage to insurgent or counterinsurgent. Marxists have won and lost as have nationalists.

INSURGENCY

Clearly defining insurgency has been almost as problematic as combating it. The U.S. Department of Defense defines insurgency as "An organized movement aimed at the overthrow of a constituted government through use of subversion and armed conflict."[8] Although strictly accurate, this definition is too broad to be helpful, and it leaves out vital characteristics. Insurgency is a hybrid form of conflict in which a clandestine organization seeks to gain control of a state from within through a combination of subversion, guerrilla warfare, and terrorism.[9] William Rosenau notes the lack of an agreed upon definition of subversion, but points out that the term generally applies to a wide range of activities employed to weaken a country by attacking key institutions with means short of armed conflict.[10] The *U.S. Government Counterinsurgency Guide,* add two other components to the definition of insurgency: propaganda and political mobilization.[11] Insurgents spread their ideological message through various media and organize people to support their cause. Mobilization usually involves a combination of persuasion and intimidation. However, a concrete biological analogy may be more useful in conveying a sense of what insurgency is than any number of academic definitions. Insurgency is like a virus: It tries to take over the body it inhabits (a country) and transforms that body to suit its own needs.

From a legal as opposed to a military perspective, insurgency is equally problematic. Insurgents have always had an ambiguous status in international law. Since the 1899 Hague Convention, the laws of war have granted belligerent rights to irregular forces, provided that they are under the command of a person responsible for their conduct, wear some type of recognizable emblem, carry arms openly, and obey the "laws and customs of war."[12] The 1949 Geneva Convention afforded the same recognition to irregular forces. Neither accord, however, addressed the status of part-time insurgent guerrillas who work by day and conduct military operations by night. In an effort to address the status of combatants and noncombatants in noninternational conflicts, the International Committee of the Red Cross (ICRC) recently issued guidance on the subject. The ICRC maintains that all persons not members of state forces or organized groups are "entitled to protection against direct attack unless and for such time as they take a direct part in hostilities."[13] Military personnel have been quick to point out that this guidance affords insurgents a "revolving door of protection" as they move from their civilian occupation to belligerent activity and back, and that it is for this reason unworkable.[14]

Academic models and legal niceties offer little practical help to soldiers, who require a functional rather than a theoretical definition. Such a definition may be derived from discussing the characteristics of insurgency, a phenomenon more easily described than precisely defined. Insurgencies arise from bad governance. A sizable segment of the population, often regionally concentrated, grows increasingly frustrated with the failure of government to perform its basic functions or angry at it for consistently exploiting them. Sometimes discontent is primarily political, especially when people see the government as the tool of a foreign power or when an ethnic minority has been oppressed by the majority. In most cases, however, social, economic, and political issues intertwine.

Discontent alone, however, is insufficient to produce insurgency. For centuries, popular rage has caused sporadic peasant revolts as renowned for their intense violence as for their utter failure to achieve any results. Insurgencies require an ideological catalyst to mobilize discontent and focus it on an achievable objective, what historian of revolution George Rudé calls "a common vocabulary of hope and protest."[15] To be effective, revolutionaries require a certain level of popular literacy and a means of disseminating their ideology. These requirements make insurgency a decidedly modern phenomenon.

In addition to ideology, insurgencies require an organization to direct their campaign against the government. The organization plans and conducts all aspects of the insurgency. It trains and equips insurgent guerrillas and decides when and where to deploy them. Traditional insurgent organizations have usually employed some form of the hub-and-spoke model. A central committee (the hub) connects to a series of cells, which vary in size and may be functionally organized for finance, logistics, etc.[16] Usually only one member of each cell serves as a link to the hub (the spoke). This model provides excellent security for clandestine organizations. Apprehension of any single insurgent usually compromises no more than one cell. Modern communications, especially mobile telephones and the Internet, have allowed for more complex organizations. Decentralized networks with a large number of nodes, some consisting of a single individual, and considerable redundancy, have increased security and made targeting insurgent organizations even more difficult.

Guerrilla warfare is a potent weapon of insurgency. The term "guerrilla," Spanish for "small war," dates to Napoleon's Peninsular Campaign. Spanish irregulars harassed French supply lines and ambushed small units, melting away in the face of superior forces. Guerrilla tactics are intended not only to wear down the government's conventional forces, but to provoke them into conducting reprisals against the general population, which they rightly or wrongly perceive as aiding the insurgents. As U.S. forces in both Iraq and Afghanistan have repeatedly encountered, insurgent guerrillas fire from occupied houses and mosques, and have no qualms about using human shields. They understand that the families of those killed and maimed will blame the security forces who return fire rather than the insurgents who initiate the attack.

Besides guerrilla warfare, insurgents also employ terror to achieve their objective of gaining power. Terror is a weapon or tactic that can be employed by many actors, each of whom uses it very differently. Its goal is to spread fear and create a sense of helplessness among those who witness a terrorist attack.

States, especially totalitarian regimes, use terror to keep their own people in line. Criminal organizations also use terror to intimidate rivals and cow their own members. Extremist organizations like al-Qaeda use terror widely and indiscriminately as part of their war against the West. Insurgents, on the other hand, use terror more selectively to avoid alienating the people whose support they wish to gain.[17] They use "enforcement" terror to instill fear in wavering supporters and employ "agitational" terror against representatives of the government and those who support it.[18] To be effective, enforcement terror has to be somewhat predictable. People need to know what behaviors will make them targets and what sort of compliance will keep them safe. Insurgents may, however, be far more willing to use agitational terror, whose limits may be determined by their capabilities. The situation in Iraq from late 2003 to 2007 illustrates the difference between insurgency and terrorism. Sunni insurgents fought to gain control of their country, using violence to that end. Al-Qaeda in Iraq wanted to keep Iraq in a state of perpetual turmoil as part of the global jihad against the West.

CHRONIC INSURGENCY AND SHADOW GOVERNANCE

Traditional insurgents fought to win. They understood that victory might take years to achieve, but they never lost sight of their ultimate objective, seizing power. A new form of insurgency has emerged in the post-Cold War world. Some insurgents recognize their inability to seize power and opt instead to carve out living space for themselves. They gain control of an area and exercise alternative or "shadow governance" over it, at times doing a better job than the official state. The weakening of state sovereignty in Asia, Africa, and Latin America has led to the proliferation of "spaces on the globe that are, for practical purposes, outside the formal international system."[19] Insurgents who carve out living space pay lip service to the idea of ultimate victory, but they fight to maintain the status quo rather than to win. Chronic insurgencies can drag on indefinitely.

COUNTERINSURGENCY

As the prefix "counter" indicates, counterinsurgency consists of those measures taken by a threatened state and its supporters to defeat an insurgency. Volumes have been written on this subject, but most good works recognize the same broad principles for conducting an effective COIN strategy.[20] The key to COIN is removing the root causes of unrest on which the insurgency feeds. Often referred to as "winning hearts and minds," this aspect of COIN consists of providing good governance. As Bernard B. Fall observed in the 1960s, a state that loses an insurgency is "not out-fought but out-governed."[21] What constitutes good governance may vary considerably with time, place, and culture. In some cases, people simply wish to be left alone and will fight anyone (insurgent or government) who threatens their traditional way of life. An ethnic minority may rebel against a government dominated by those from another group. And of course, people frequently rebel against foreign occupation.

Developing an effective COIN strategy requires correctly ascertaining the causes upon which the insurgency feeds. This determination in turn necessitates listening to local people. Too often an intervening power has presumed to know best what the people it seeks to help really need. The U.S. emphasis on elections is a case in point. "The West came into Afghanistan under the mantra of freedom is on the march," observed Masood Farviar, manager of an Afghan radio network in a December 2010 interview with National Public Radio, "and elections are the cure-all for all the problems, without realizing that the last thing Afghans needed at the time was elections. And the first thing Afghans needed at the time was security."[22] In its rush to get a government in place—any government—the United States got one with little legitimacy or real power. A popular joke in Afghanistan has it that Hamid Karzai is supposed to be president but is really no more than the mayor of Kabul, and even that only until it is dark.

The same preoccupation with quick elections occurred in Iraq. As Michael Gordon and General Bernard Trainor convincingly demonstrate in *Cobra II*, the White House's emphasis on elections at the expense of reconstruction and security not only allowed the insurgency to develop but has hampered efforts to counter it ever since.[23] An incident following the Second Battle of Fallujah graphically illustrated the problem with this approach. Following recapture of the city, a member of the Interim Governing Council told a group of its citizens that they had been liberated and could now have elections. Ignoring his proclamation of this good news, they demanded to know when the electric and water service would be restored, when trash would be collected, etc.

The reaction of the citizens of Fallujah illustrates another important point about winning hearts and minds. According to Abraham Maslow's "hierarchy

of needs," security comes well ahead of "self actu-
alization," which includes political participation.[24]
While most people do not expect their government to
meet all or even most of the basic needs Maslow defines, they do want it to safeguard and even facilitate
their ability to acquire the necessities of life through
their own efforts. Economic grievances have been a
major cause of most insurgencies, even those that purported to be about something else. Road building in
Afghanistan illustrates how good governance should
work. Roads link villages to towns and cities, providing people access to markets for their produce. Hiring
local people to build the roads also creates jobs, and,
because it benefits them directly, the locals will also
defend the road from Taliban attack.[25]

Politics does, of course, matter. People who already
have the necessities of life but lack political rights may
rebel if they feel excluded from or marginalized in the
political life of the nation. Only by creating avenues
for legitimate political participation can such a state
prevent people seeking an alternative through insurgency. When a foreign power intervenes to remove an
oppressive government, free and democratic elections
should be held as soon as possible. To hold them before providing adequate security and restoring basic
government services, however, may be ill-advised.

While it addresses roots causes of unrest, a COIN
campaign must also combat insurgent guerrillas and
terrorists. Deadly force plays an important but limited
role in COIN. A threatened state must, however, make
sure its use of force remains focused and proportional,
or it risks alienating people and driving them into the
arms of the insurgents. The security forces, consisting
of police and military, protect vulnerable targets and
attack insurgent fighters and the organization they

represent. In so doing, they create a shield behind which the hearts-and-minds campaign occurs.

Using force in a focused, appropriate manner requires good intelligence. Only by knowing who the insurgents are can the security forces target them without causing unnecessary casualties among the general population in which the insurgents hide. The best intelligence comes not from covert operations or coerced testimony of captured insurgents, but from voluntary cooperation of people persuaded that the government can protect them, is capable of reform, and will serve them better than the insurgents. Some intelligence must be operationally generated through a process that turns "background information into contact information."[26]

Since insurgents rarely operate in large groups, large conventional military formations do not function well in combating them. Platoons and even section are far more effective at COIN than companies and battalions. For this reason, junior officers and senior noncommissioned officers (NCOs) must be trained and equipped to fight insurgents and encouraged to take initiative in doing so. The U.S. military describes this approach as "empowering the lowest levels," what in conventional war the Germans call "auftragstaktik."[27] Traditional COIN literature speaks of the need to educate and train "strategic corporals," NCOs who understand the nature of COIN and the impact tactical actions have on strategy.

COIN requires the use of all elements of national power, what U.S. doctrine calls the DIMEFIL: diplomatic, information, military, economic, financial, intelligence, and law enforcement.[28] Achieving unity of effort among the disparate government departments, the military, and the police implementing these elements of strategy is very important but extremely difficult. Using these elements to support a threatened government which the supporting power does not control is even harder, but such is the role the United States currently plays and is likely to play for the foreseeable future.

HISTORICAL ANALYSIS: FOUR DIFFERENT OUTCOMES

Group 1: Insurgent Victories.

The period 1945-70 saw the highest concentration of insurgencies to date. The prevalence of these conflicts derived from a unique set of circumstances following World War II. In 1945, European powers still controlled most of Africa and much of Asia. However, the war had weakened them, and the Japanese had proven that Western armies could be defeated by non-Western ones. Nationalist movements gained strength as European power waned. Efforts to reassert colonial control met with stiff resistance. Nationalist insurgencies drove the French from Indochina, the Dutch from Indonesia, and the Belgians from the Congo. This string of victories led some observers to conclude that insurgency was an irresistible form of warfare.[29] Other analysts attributed the insurgents' success to the "soft" colonial governments they opposed.[30] These writers argued, correctly as it turned out, that in the future insurgents would have a much more difficult time.

Three conflicts in particular commend themselves as good examples of decisive insurgent victories. From 1944-47, Zionist insurgents drove the British from Palestine and established the state of Israel. From 1954 to 1962, nationalist insurgents forced the French from Algeria. Both conflicts blended urban with rural guerrilla warfare. In each case, the insurgents won, not by defeating the government militarily but by making the cost of continuing the struggle unacceptably high. International opinion also played a role in deciding each conflict as did outside support for the insurgency. The third case occurred in the recent past. From 1997 to 1999, the Kosovo Liberation Army conducted an effective insurgency against the government of Yugoslavia (by then reduced to Serbia and Montenegro). In this case, however, the insurgents did not persuade the hated government to abdicate, but instead induced a coalition of powers to intervene on its behalf, producing the same result, independence for the province.

Palestine. Britain gained control of what became the states of Jordan and Israel as part of the peace settlement that ended World War I. The newly created League of Nations granted them the territory as a Mandate, an area to be governed and developed by the United Kingdom (UK) under loose supervision by the League of Nations. To further complicate matters, Britain had to reconcile its colonial ambitions with commitments made to Arabs and Jews during the war. The McMahon-Hussein correspondence of 1915-16 had promised the sons of Hussein, the Sharif of Mecca, Arab kingdoms as a reward for revolting against Britain's enemy, the Ottoman Empire.[31] In 1917, British Foreign Secretary Arthur James Balfour issued the famous Balfour Declaration promising the "establishment of a national home for the Jewish people in Palestine."[32] While making these conflicting promises, the British government entered into the Sykes-Picot Agreement (1916), dividing the Middle East with France.[33]

Britain resolved its commitment to the Sharif of Mecca with the less than satisfactory expedient of setting up his first son, Feisal, as King of Iraq (another Ottoman territory acquired from the Turks) and his second son, Hussein, as Emir (later king) of Transjordan (carved out of the eastern part of the Mandate of Palestine), both British client states. To honor its pledge to the Zionists, the British agreed to facilitate Jewish immigration to Palestine through the Jewish Agency, the official Zionist organization created for that purpose. The influx of Jewish immigrants angered Palestinian Arabs, produced intercommunal conflict, and led to a full-scale Arab Revolt from 1936 to 1939. The British suppressed the revolt but promised to limit further Jewish immigration to 75,000 over the next 5 years, after which no more Jews would be allowed to enter the Mandate without Arab approval.[34] The Zionists considered this decision tantamount to handing Palestine to the Arabs. They bided their time until World War II ended, and even fought alongside the British to defeat Germany. Then they revolted against British rule.

The Zionist confronted Britain with a complex insurgency perpetrated by three organizations clandestinely linked to the official Jewish Agency. The *Irgun Haganah Ha'ivrith Be Eretz Israel* (Hebrew Defense Organization in Palestine), or "Haganah" for short, had formed in 1921 to protect Jewish settlements from Arab attack and was tacitly allowed by the colonial administration, and may even have received arms from the British.[35] A second, more militant group, the *Irgun Zvei Lumi* (National Military Organization) broke with the Haganah in 1931 and conducted reprisals against the Arabs during the 1936-39 Arab Revolt.[36] The third group, *Lochmei Heruth Israel* (Fighters for the Freedom of Israel), better known as the "Stern Gang" for its founder, Avram Stern, was the most militant. The Haganah numbered 45,000; the Irgun, 1,500; and the Stern Gang, 300.[37]

The three groups cooperated to conduct a highly effective insurgency against the British Army. They sabotaged rail lines, assassinated members of the security forces, and bombed government buildings, most notably the King David Hotel in July 1946. The British replied with tried-and-true colonial methods. They promulgated emergency regulations that allowed them to detain suspects without trial, conducted massive cordon-and-search operations, and imposed economic sanctions on the Jewish community.[38] While these measures had a salutary effect on the security situation, they proved unsustainable. In the end the insurgents won, not by defeating the security forces, but by persuading the British government that nothing in Palestine warranted the continued expenditure in British blood and treasure necessary to retain the territory.

Insurgent victory derived from the failure of the British government to win any support among the Jewish population of Palestine. Nothing short of a Zionist state would satisfy them, and Britain could not deliver on this demand given its commitments to the Palestinian Arabs and to other Arab states. Without this political offer to win some degree of popular support, the security forces could not garner the intelligence necessary for them to defeat the insurgents. "The reason we catch no terrorists," concluded then Commander-in-Chief Middle East Land Forces General Sir Miles Dempsey, "is that the people of this country take no action either directly or in giving evidence."[39] Repression alone might have sufficed had the insurgency been isolated. However, the Zionists had a powerful ally in the person of President Harry Truman. Eager to secure the Jewish vote in major states like New York during the 1946 midterm elections, Truman pressured the British to allow Holocaust survivors to immigrate to Palestine and to relax security measures within the Mandate. Increasingly dependent on U.S. aid to recover from World War II, Britain had no choice but to comply.

Algeria. The French encountered a similar colonial dilemma in Algeria. Acquired in 1830 and governed by its European population as a Department of France with representatives in Paris, the North African territory became the centerpiece of the country's colonial empire. By the middle of the 20th century, approximately 1 million French Algerians (known as Colons or *Pied Noir*, Black Feet) dominated a population of 8 million indigenous people.[40] Nationalism developed in Algeria as it did throughout the colonial world during the first decades of the 20th century. Despite their desire for independence or at least greater political rights, however, many indigenous Algerians supported France during World War II, expecting to be rewarded for their loyalty. France answered their demand for inclusion with a proposal to grant citizenship to a small percentage of native people based on a merit system. Nationalists answered this proposal with a large-scale protest in 1945, which the French suppressed with considerable loss of life. In 1954, various resistance groups united to form the National Liberation Front (NLF), which launched an insurgency leading to independence following a bloody 8-year struggle. However, NLF success owed more to French COIN and the political crisis it created at home than it did to insurgent prowess. The French military won most of the battles but in the process lost the war.

From 1954 to 1957, the NLF enjoyed considerable success. The organization recruited 40,000 fighters for its military wing, the National Liberation Army (NLA).[41] It benefited from a wave of nationalism sweeping the Middle East and Africa. When its neighbors, Tunisia and Morocco, received independence, the insurgents enjoyed safe havens on their territory and a source of supply. Although it enjoyed little popular support at the outset, the NLF employed the classic insurgent tactic of provoking the government into over-reacting to its attacks. The NLA assassinated pro-French Muslims and murdered Colons. The French Army gave the civilians weapons to protect themselves, which led inevitably to them conducting reprisals against Algerian Muslims innocent of any wrongdoing. These reprisals widened support for the insurgents as did the NLF's own campaign of intimidation and coercion.[42] The situation deteriorated as France poured in more and more troops, which reached a total of 500,000, most deployed in static defensive positions.[43]

Beginning in 1957, the security forces reversed the deteriorating situation, systematically degrading the NLF and NLA and maintaining the military initiative until the end of the war. Contrary to popular perceptions, the French COIN campaign consisted of far more than systematic brutality, though security force excesses did cost the army its legitimacy and ultimately lost it the war. The army divided rural Algeria into operational areas, relocated threatened villages, and conducted extensive and long-lasting sweeps to disrupt the NLA. While living conditions in most *regroupment* areas were poor, at least some French officials tried to use the process as an instrument of economic and social development.[44] The army placed companies of soldiers within threatened villages, where they bonded with local people, and created indigenous defense forces. They also constructed along the Tunisian border a defensive line backed by artillery and mobile forces.

None of these effective measures or any combination of them, however, could offset the damage to French legitimacy done by the brutal tactics of the army. Nowhere were these excesses more clearly demonstrated than in the infamous Battle of Algiers. Beginning in January 1957, forces under the command of General Massau moved to destroy the NLF network in Algiers. They conducted a detailed census of all households, divided the Muslim areas into sectors, imposed population movement controls, and rounded up thousands of suspects. Through the systematic use of torture, the army gained precise intelligence on the insurgent order of battle, assembling a detailed organizational chart called an *organogram*. This operation destroyed the NLF in the capital in a matter of weeks, although a second follow-up operation had to be mounted to disrupt efforts to rebuild it.[45]

The war in Algeria led to a major political crisis in metropolitan France. The Fourth Republic fell over its failure to bring the conflict to a successful conclusion. Charles de Gaulle returned to power in May 1958 amid expectations by the army that he would support strong measures against the insurgents. The new French constitution strengthened the office of president, perhaps in the hope that doing so would enable de Gaulle to end the crisis. However, rather than continue the war, de Gaulle conducted a referendum in which the Algerians voted for independence. Some generals attempted a coup in April 1961, and when that failed, they formed a clandestine organization and conducted their own terrorist campaign. The French people, however, had become more upset by the conduct of their own army than they were with the behavior of the insurgents and would not support continuing the war. The Evian Accords negotiated with the NLF gave Algeria independence in March 1962.

Kosovo. While most insurgent successes occurred during the era of decolonization, a more recent campaign illustrates that insurgents can occasionally achieve decisive victory even in the contemporary world. The insurgency conducted by Kosovar Albanians against the government of Yugoslavia (by then reduced to Serbia and Montenegro) resulted in intervention by the North Atlantic Treaty Organization (NATO), which forced Yugoslavia to withdraw and led to independence for the Province. As with the campaigns in Palestine and Algeria, the insurgents could not hope to defeat the government militarily, but once again, they did not have to do so. Like the NLF in Algeria, the Kosovo insurgents provoked the Yugoslav government into a policy of brutal reprisals that cost it what little legitimacy it had left, produced international criticism, and provoked outside intervention.

The Kingdom of Serbia acquired Kosovo following the second Balkan War in 1913. Despite its fertile soil and considerable mineral wealth, it was the poorest province of the former Yugoslavia. By 1991, the year of the last Yugoslav census, ethnic Albanians comprised 82 percent of the population; Serbians, 10 percent; and Roma and others, the remaining 8 percent.[46] Most Kosovar Albanians practiced a relaxed form of Islam, which along with language and ethnicity separated them from their Slav orthodox Serbian neighbors. While most Serbians lived in small islands amid a sea of Albanians, they formed the majority in the region north of the city of Mitrovica.

A decade before its own insurgent movement struggled for independence, Kosovo had played a pivotal role in the breakup of Yugoslavia. In 1989, Serbian leader Slobodan Milosevic spoke at the historic site of the 1389 battle of Kosovo Polje (Field of Black Birds) and declared the province to be the cradle of Serbian civilization. He revoked Kosovo's autonomy and began a policy of removing Albanians from key positions in local government and the economy, relegating them to the status of a permanent underclass. Fear of such Serbian domination encouraged separatist movements in other parts of Yugoslavia. The declaration of independence by Slovenia, followed by wars in Croatia and Bosnia, kept the international community occupied for much of the next decade, and Kosovo fell off the front page.

Isolated geographically and with little outside support, Kosovar Albanians had few options. With open resistance out of the question, Ibrahim Rugova led a nonviolent movement to create a parallel state providing health, education, and welfare benefits for Kosavars.[47] The situation changed dramatically in 1997. The government in neighboring Albania collapsed following a financial crisis, losing control of some of its military arsenals in the process. Contraband weapons poured into Kosovo, enabling a fringe group to form in 1993 (the Kosovo Liberation Army [KLA]) and to mount an armed struggle against the Serbian regime. Beginning in the fall of 1997, the KLA launched an assassination campaign against Serbian police, government officials, and Albanian collaborators, which in turn provoked the kind of reprisals against the general Albanian population the insurgents desired and

Rugova feared.[48] In February 1998, the Yugoslav army and Serbian paramilitaries launched an offensive in the Drenica region, which killed 51 people, including 23 women and 11 children; in the ensuing weeks, another 85 Kosavars were murdered.[49] As many as 250,000 people fled the Drenica Region, sparking international fears of a new wave of ethnic cleansing.[50]

The United States and its NATO allies were unwilling to witness a repeat of the Bosnian tragedy. Amid escalating violence, the United States led the alliance in a 78-day air campaign that ultimately forced Serbian withdrawal from the province. After several years in political limbo as a United Nations (UN) and NATO protectorate, Kosovo became an independent nation in 2008. The insurgency had achieved its objective. The new country will require economic support and security assistance for years to come, but renewed fighting seems unlikely.

How Insurgents Can Win. These three cases clearly indicate the circumstance under which insurgents might achieve a decisive victory. In each case, the government was seen by the majority of people as an occupying power with little legitimacy, and the COIN methods it employed further damaged its cause. The League of Nations Mandate put a fig leaf of decency over colonial rule in Palestine. Algeria's status as a Department of metropolitan France did not alter the fact that a minority of French Colons governed a native majority who had few political rights. Although it had been an autonomous province of Serbia in old Yugoslavia, Kosovo lost its political status when Milosevic came to power. Its Albanian majority then suffered discrimination similar to that endured by colonial subjects. Historical and contemporary examples thus support J. Bowyer Bell's conclusion that insurgents have been most successful against "soft" colonial targets.[51]

However, the unpopularity of a colonial or neo-colonial government alone, no matter how oppressive, does not guarantee an insurgency's success. Despite facing stiff resistance over a decade, the Russian Federation eventually crushed the Chechen separatist movement. China has had little difficulty suppressing opposition from its Uyghur minority. In these cases, two conditions absent in Palestine, Algeria, and Kosovo explain the insurgents' failure: political will and lack of outside support. Both the Russian Federation and China consider maintaining control over the threatened areas vital to their national interest. Chechnya's location in the oil rich north Caucasus region makes it too valuable a piece of real estate to lose. If China allowed one minority population to secede, others might follow. Both governments thus have had ample political will to continue the struggle whatever the cost. Besides facing a determined, powerful state, the insurgents could count on neither direct support nor international pressure to help them. Humanitarian groups might condemn the repression, but no state or coalition considered intervening even covertly in the internal affairs of either Russia or China.

In the cases of Palestine, Algeria, and Kosovo very different circumstances prevailed. Neither the British government nor its public considered retaining control over Palestine crucial to the survival of the empire, never mind the state. Nothing the territory offered was worth the cost in blood, treasure, and international ill-will of fighting to keep it. The Zionists also benefited from outside support. The Holocaust generated great sympathy for their cause, and they received financial support from the American Jewish community. The Democratic Party needed Jewish votes in key states like New York in the 1946 congressional and 1948 presidential elections. Britain needed American aide to rebuild its economy and was amenable to pressure from the Truman administration to allow more Jewish refugees into Palestine.

While the French Army considered the loss of Algeria unacceptable, the French public did not. Contrary to what Francois Mitterrand asserted, Algeria was not France. Having suffered persecution under Nazi occupation, ordinary French people deplored the brutal measures being used to keep the territory. International opinion condemned French colonialism, but it is unclear what if any role such condemnation played in the decision to withdraw. The Algerian insurgents also enjoyed a safe haven across the Tunisian and Moroccan borders. In the final analysis, the cost to France of remaining in Algeria in blood, treasure, and perhaps moral capital as well became unacceptably high. Under these circumstances, the time had come to go.

In Kosovo, the insurgency followed a different course. Serbia had both the political will and the military power to retain control of its southern province indefinitely. However, in this conflict, international disapproval led to direct intervention. The KLA provoked the Yugoslav police, military and Serbian paramilitaries into heavy handed tactics, including the use of rape and ethnic cleansing as had been perpetrated in Bosnia. By 1999, the international community in general and the West in particular had enough of such gross human rights violations. NATO, led by the United States, launched a 78-day air campaign to force Serbian withdrawal from the province. For the next decade, Kosovo remained in limbo as talks over its status continued. Finally, in February 2008, it declared independence and was recognized by the United States and some of the NATO allies.

The circumstances under which insurgents win outright victories are thus quite specific. The government they oppose is seen as a foreign occupier, which lacks popular support and faces international criticism. Domestic opinion in the occupier's home country wanes as the cost of colonial or neocolonial control rises. The insurgents enjoy material support from outside the contested territory and/or a safe haven in a neighboring country. In some cases, a foreign power or coalition intervenes on behalf of the insurgents. A confluence of such circumstances rarely occurs, which is why insurgent victories outside the era of decolonization have been few.

Group 2: Government Victories.

If outright insurgent victories seldom occur, unequivocal government triumphs are equally rare. At the turn of the 20th century, the U.S. Army defeated an insurrection in the Philippines. In the 1950s, U.S. forces returned to the Philippines to help its government defeat the Communist Hukbalahap revolt. In the 1960s, the Bolivian government defeated an abortive Communist insurgency led by Cuban revolutionary hero, Che Guevara. However, three other cases commend themselves as the best examples of the highly favorable conditions under which a threatened government can win: the Malayan Emergency (1948-60), the Greek Civil War (1946-49), and the Tamil insurgency in Sri Lanka (1983-2009).

Malaya. The Malayan Emergency has long been hailed as the textbook case of effective COIN. From 1948 to 1960, the British defeated a well-armed and organized Communist insurgency. While the exact number of insurgents will never be known, the British estimated around 6,500 active fighters with perhaps as many as 50,000 supporters from a total population of just over 4.3 million.[52] The insurgent guerrillas had been trained by the British to fight the Japanese and knew the terrain very well. While the insurgency remained confined to the ethnic minority Chinese, this group still comprised 38 percent of the Malayan population.

After a few years of trial and error, the British employed effective COIN methods they had developed during a century of policing their empire. They based their strategy on four broad principles: winning the hearts and minds of disaffected people, keeping the use of force against the insurgents limited and focused, decentralizing command and control, and achieving unity of effort between the civil and military sides of the operation.[53] At the same time, they trained and equipped the Malayan police and military to take over security operations after Britain granted the colony independence and continued to lend it support for years to come.

The British strategy was dubbed the Briggs plan for the Director of Operations, Sir Harold Briggs. Briggs and his staff understood that the key to victory lay in separating the insurgent cadres operating in the jungles from their supporters among the Chinese population living in squatter villages along the jungle fringe. The squatters had a low standard of living, lacking both Malayan citizenship and title to the land they occupied. Discontent reinforced by intimidation encouraged them to support the insurgents. The Briggs plan relocated the squatters away from the jungle fringe to "new villages," which could be more easily protected. Because the new villages usually offered better housing, running water, schools, clinics, and other amenities, most Chinese willingly moved to them. Those who refused to move, the British relocated by force.[54] The program proved so successful, that all but six of the 480 new villages survived as permanent communities after the war.[55]

The Briggs plan laid the foundation for successful COIN in Malaya. Relocation, Briggs noted, was not in itself a solution, but it did provide "that measure of protection and concentration which makes good administration possible."[56] Controlling the population allowed the security forces to reduce the insurgents' food supply. It also improved intelligence gathering, as people are more likely to talk if the government can protect them. Improved intelligence allowed the army to use force in a more focused manner.

Effective COIN requires unity of effort. At the local level, three key officials (the police chief, the army battalion commander, and the District Commissioner) had to work closely together. To facilitate cooperation, the British created a system of emergency committees from District to State to Federation level. The appointment of General (later Field Marshall) Sir Gerald Templer as both High Commissioner and Director of Operations (DO) achieved unity of effort at the top, which had been lacking under Briggs, who held only the DO position. Templer energized the campaign. He insisted that every District Emergency Committee meet at least once a day, "if only to have a whiskey and soda in the evening."[57]

The final ingredient of successful COIN was decentralization of command and control, what the U.S. military now calls "empowering the lowest levels."[58] Large conventional formations are worse than useless in pursuing guerrillas who melt away before them. Platoons or even sections can hunt them far more effectively. However, small unit operations can only succeed if senior commanders delegate responsibility, which British commanders proved willing to do. "The only thing a divisional commander has to do in this sort of war," quipped one brigadier, "is to go around seeing that the troops have got their beer."[59] To further enhance effectiveness of small unit tactics, the British used "framework deployment," assigning a battalion to a single area for an extended period of time so that soldiers could get to know its terrain and people.

Impressive though the Malayan campaign was, it would be a mistake to overlook British advantages in waging it. Malaya was a valuable piece of real estate worth defending for its resources and strategic location. Rubber production funded much of the COIN campaign. The insurgency remained confined to the minority Chinese population, who could be won over with offers of citizenship and land. Despite their Communist affiliation, the insurgents received no outside support, nor did they enjoy a safe haven, since Malaya's one land border (with Thailand) was too remote and inhospitable to provide access to sanctuary. As colonial masters, the British could also use draconian measures that would be unacceptable to a democratic state in today's climate of transparency. Together with its allies, Britain saw the campaign as an anti-Communist crusade, not colonial oppression. Furthermore, internal conflict did not end with British withdrawal. Malaysia faced a decade more of strife, which included insurgency in North Borneo, a cross border war with Indonesia, and the amicable split with Singapore. These advantages notwithstanding, the British approach to COIN has much to commend it and continues to be worth studying.

Greece. Although the United States had no formal empire, it did control territory in the Pacific and behaved in a paternal manner towards the governments of small nations in the Caribbean and Central America, its self-proclaimed sphere of influence. From 1900 to 1940, it faced insurgent conflicts in these areas. Unfortunately, much of the wisdom gained in these operations was lost when the military developed into a massive conventional force to fight World War II. During the Cold War, American forces once again engaged in COIN, supporting states threatened by Communist revolution.

The first such conflict occurred in Greece (1946-49), where a Communist insurgency with more than 50,000 fighters vied for control of the country amid the chaos at the end of World War II. The British liberated the country from the Axis, attempted to disarm all guerrilla bands, and supported a pro-Western government. However, fiscal constraints forced Britain to end its support of the Greek government in March 1947. With Communist governments controlling Yugoslavia, Albania, Hungary, Romania, and Bulgaria, Greece looked to be the last bastion of democracy in southeastern Europe.

Determined that the country should not fall, President Harry Truman provided $723.6 million in aid plus 800 military and 700 civilian advisors.[60] The Americans pursued a conventional approach to COIN, insisting that the infantry move in to fix the enemy so that artillery could destroy them, although they also criticized Greek forces for indiscriminate firing, which killed innocent civilians.[61] This conventional approach, which under different circumstances would have cost the government popular support, succeeded largely because of insurgent mistakes and fortuitous circumstances. Much of the fighting occurred in remote mountainous areas where excesses went largely unnoticed. In addition, the insurgents accepted battle on terms favorable to the government. Believing that the time was right for large-scale operations, they reorganized their forces from small bands of 50 to 100 into "brigades" and "divisions."[62] These larger formations could be more easily targeted by the Greek Army supported by the Americans. The following year, the Communist government of Yugoslavia quarreled with the Kremlin and closed its border to the insurgents, depriving them of the safe havens and supply bases they had enjoyed. Finally, the kidnapping of thousand of Greek children to be "educated" in Communist countries cost the insurgents popular support. Thus, with minimal attention to winning hearts and minds, the Greek government achieved a conventional military victory over an unconventional foe. From this "success" story, the U.S. military drew the mistaken conclusion that conventional methods could counter unconventional threats.

Liberation Tigers of Tamil Eelam. The third example of a clear-cut government victory occurred in Sri Lanka, where the Singhalese-led government fought a 26-year war with the Liberation Tigers of Tamil Eelam (LTTE). The Tamils are a Hindu ethnic group from Southern India who comprise 10 percent of Sri Lanka's 21 million people. The majority Singhalese population considered that the Tamils had collaborated with the British, who ruled the island as Ceylon.[63] They thus discriminated against the Tamils when the colony gained independence in 1948. The new state made Singhalese the official language (excluding Tamil) and disenfranchised Tamil migrants from India. In response to this discrimination, Velupillai Prabhakaran created the LTTE (successor to another insurgent group, the Tamil New Tigers) in 1976 to campaign for a Tamil homeland. The conflict began in 1983 when the LTTE ambushed an army convoy, killing 13 soldiers; 2,500 Tamils died in subsequent retaliatory riots.[64]

The LTTE soon gained control of large areas in northern and eastern Sri Lanka. In the process, Prabhakaran eliminated other Tamil resistance leaders and imposed tight control over the Tamil community. The LTTE became a parallel state, exercising shadow governance in the territories it controlled. It developed police, judicial, and economic institutions and ran its own schools.[65] The Tigers also had perhaps the most impressive financial network of any insurgent group. Most of its money came from the 600-800,000 member Tamil diaspora community through a combination of voluntary contributions and extortion. North Korea may also have supplied the LTTE with arms and training. Even when international efforts led to a 70 percent decline in foreign funding, the organization still managed to raise $200-300 million per year from its licit and illicit businesses.[66]

These resources allowed the LTTE to create an impressive military force. At its height, the insurgents could field as many as 15,000 fighters, of whom 7,000 were combat trained.[67] It had an impressive arsenal of weapons, including long-range artillery, and captured armored vehicles as well as mortars and small arms.[68] The LTTE even had a small naval wing, the Sea Tigers. With its formidable arsenal and extensive resources, the LTTE proved capable of defending most Tamil areas.

The insurgents also took the fight to the government and its allies through a highly effective terrorist campaign. They assassinated several high-ranking officials, including Indian Prime Minister Rajiv Gandhi, whose troops had intervened against the Tamils

(1991), Sri Lankan President Ranasinghe Premadasa (1993), and the Sri Lankan Industry and Foreign Ministers (2000 and 2005). The LTTE proved particularly adept at suicide operations, developing a dedicated cadre, the Black Tigers, specifically for the purpose. The Black Tigers pioneered the suicide vest, a garment packed with plastic explosives and shrapnel (often ball bearings).[69] They frequently used women as suicide bombers; the women could carry a larger payload by feigning pregnancy, knowing men would be reluctant to search them.

Like the Greeks, the Sri Lankans took a largely conventional approach to their unconventional conflict. Wining hearts and minds proved extremely difficult once the violence escalated. Besides limited local autonomy, a threatened state has little to offer an ethnic separatist movement that wishes to dismember the nation. Had the 1948 constitution granted the Tamils even limited local autonomy and use of their language, however, the insurgency might never have occurred. By the 1980s, these concessions no longer satisfied Tamil aspirations. The Singhalese would not compromise the territorial integrity of the state, and the LTTE had the resources and popular support to defend and even govern its enclaves. Under these circumstances, the conflict consisted of periods of intense fighting interspersed with uneasy truces amid a steady stream of terrorist attacks. Indian intervention in the mid-1980s accomplished nothing on the ground, but did provoke the assassination of Indian Prime Minister Rajiv Gandhi in 1991. Both the government and the insurgents, meanwhile, racked up a long list of human rights violations.

Over time, however, circumstances changed in favor of the government. The LTTE had never garnered support or legitimacy outside Sri Lanka and its own diaspora community. Tolerance for terrorism in any form plummeted after September 11, 2001 (9/11), and concerted attacks upon terrorist financing hurt the Tigers. More importantly, heavy handed tactics began to erode the LTTE's support base in the Tamil population, especially as the Singhalese government became more attentive to human rights and more willing to engage in meaningful reform. An insurgency that uses more terror to keep its own people in line than it does in fighting the government is on its way to defeat. The LTTE also suffered from the fatal weakness of over-reliance on a charismatic but dictatorial leader. During the first decade of the new century, the government in Colombo exploited these weaknesses, working with dissident groups in the Tamil community. More and more Tamils fled south to Singhalese territory to escape Prabhakaran's brutal rule.

A July 2009 interview with a top LTTE commander who defected in 2006 reveals growing problems within the organization. Colonel Karuna Amman had been one of Prabhakaran's body guards and advanced to second-in-command of the organization's armed forces. As commander of the Tigers' eastern enclave, Karuna led a force of 6,000 Tamil fighters. When he disbanded his troops and defected to the government, he left the province vulnerable to capture by the Sri Lankan Army in 2007. A mixture of Prabhakaran's rigid rules and personal cowardice (he always stayed away from the fighting), disillusioned Karuna as did the leader's intransigence. Karuna said he had opposed the assassination of Rajiv Gandhi because it brought international condemnation on what had been until then a Tamil liberation movement. Finally, he explained, despite growing signs that the LTTE could never win a military victory, Prabhakaran refused to seriously pursue a political settlement.[70]

The dénouement came with the Sri Lankan Army's northern offensive of 2008-09. In January 2009, the army captured the LTTE "capital" of Kilinochchi. They squeezed the remaining Tigers into a smaller and smaller area in the Northeast, which they systematically decimated with artillery. Human rights groups and the UN condemned the Sri Lankan army for indiscriminate shelling but were equally critical of the LTTE for using the trapped population as human shields. The LTTE fighters shot civilians trying to flee the combat zone. In May, the Sri Lankan Army killed Prabhakaran and several of his associates as they sought to escape. Other LTTE leaders committed suicide. The remaining Tigers laid down their arms, and the 26-year conflict came to a close.

Defeating Insurgents. Drawn from different times and regions, the three cases in this group offer some compelling conclusions. Governments win outright victories over insurgents only under very favorable circumstances. All three insurgencies occurred in geographically isolated areas. Malaya is a peninsula with dense jungles along its only land border. Sri Lanka is an island. Greece is a peninsula that became a virtual island for the insurgents once Yugoslavia closed its borders to them. Insurgent disadvantages and/or outright mistakes further contributed to government success. The Malayan Peoples Liberation Army was confined to the Chinese minority community as the LTTE was to the Tamil. Greek insurgents accepted battle on terms favorable to the Greek Army, trained and equipped by the United States. All three insurgent groups exploited people in the areas they controlled. The LTTE was exceptionally brutal, and the Greek insurgents kidnapped thousand of Greek children whom they sent to Communist countries for "education." The LTTE had the added disadvantage of reliance on a charismatic leader, who could not be easily replaced. Threatened governments can seldom count on such favorable circumstances. Thus while the three cases in this group yield valuable operational and tactical lessons, they are not suitable models for contemporary COIN strategists.

Group 3: Degenerate Insurgencies.

Insurgency has a shelf life—it succeeds, fails, or degenerates into something else. As previously noted, most unconditional insurgent victories belong to the era of decolonization, and the few clear-cut government victories occurred under a very specific combination of circumstances that seldom occur. Insurgent movements that fail to achieve their goals and yet avoid defeat sometimes degenerate into mere extremist organizations, capable of carrying out terrorist attacks but of doing little else, or they morph into criminality. The Basque separatist organization, Fatherland and Liberty, illustrates the former case, while Peru's Shining Path and Colombia's narco-insurgency, Revolutionary Armed Forces of Colombia (FARC), illustrate the latter.

The Basque Separatist Movement. The Basque separatist movement (ETA) began in much the same way as the LTTE. The 20,664 square kilometer Basque region straddles the Pyrenees. Approximately two-thirds of this territory and most of the region's 3 million people are part of Spain; the remaining people and territory belong to France. Because the Basques backed the Republicans in the Spanish Civil War (1936-39), the fascist dictator Francisco Franco systematically oppressed them when he came to power, banning their language, suppressing their culture, and arresting their intellectuals.[71]

Discouraged by the failure of nonviolent protest to achieve reform, the Basques launched an insurgency against the Spanish government. ETA's active strength probably numbered in the hundreds during its heyday, with thousands more supporters.[72] The ability of the organization to rapidly replace losses suggests that its active deployment reflected the optimum number of fighters for the combat environment rather than limits on its ability to recruit. Beginning in the 1960s, ETA attacked police and other government employees, first in the Basque region itself and then in the Spanish capital of Madrid. The group achieved its most dramatic success by assassinating Franco's hand-picked successor, Admiral Luis Carrero Blanco, with a bomb placed under his car in 1973. Many Spaniards quietly approved the killing, sharing the joke that the admiral was Spain's first astronaut.

The insurgents' greatest achievement also started a chain of events that led to its decline. Franco never found another suitable successor. Following his death in 1975 and restoration of the monarchy, democracy returned to Spain. A new constitution (1978) addressed most Basque grievances, granting the region limited autonomy, allowing use of the Basque language for official purposes, and restoring cultural institutions. However, these concessions did not satisfy ETA, which continued its campaign of violence. With the authoritarian regime removed, the movement launched its most intensive wave of attacks after reform had progressed considerably.[73] ETA's deadliest year was 1980, during which it killed 76 people.[74] The pattern of attacks also changed. Previously the group had targeted police, military, and government officials in classic insurgent fashion. Now it targeted innocent civilians. In its most infamous attack, ETA bombed a Barcelona shopping mall in 1987, killing 21 people.

The Franco regime had seen no need to mount a COIN campaign. Repression kept ETA in check and, while the group garnered sympathy, it had no real support outside the Basque provinces. The restoration of democracy weakened the oppressive instruments of state control and necessitated a more sophisticated response to the insurgency. Concessions to Basque nationalism formed a major part of the new approach. Madrid granted the province limited local autonomy, restored universities and cultural institutions, and permitted use of the Basque language. The government also went on the offensive. ETA had long benefited from its safe haven in the French Basque region. During the Franco era, Republican France had been disinclined to cooperate with fascist Spain. The situation did not improve significantly after Franco's death, so the Spanish resorted to extra-legal covert operations. The *Grupo Antiterrorista de Liberación* (Anti-terrorist Liberation Group, or GAL) assassinated suspected terrorists in the Spanish and French Basque regions, killing 27 people in 25 attacks.[75] GAL, one of several such groups, turned out to be sponsored by the Spanish Interior Ministry.[76] Although GAL death squads drew widespread criticism, they did encourage France to abandon its policy of tacitly allowing ETA to operate within its territory. Paris and Madrid signed an extradition treaty depriving ETA of its safe haven in Basque territory across the Pyrenees. They later agreed to allow hot pursuit of suspects by French and Spanish police 60 kilometers on either side of the border. Within Spain, a government crackdown reduced the organization's effectiveness. ETA declared a ceasefire in 1998, and many considered the insurgency over. The Madrid train bombings of March 11, 2004, raised the disturbing possibility that a new generation of ETA members had cooperated with al-Qaeda. However, no evidence of such a connection has ever been produced. ETA violence has been reduced to sporadic attacks within the Basque Province.

Most analysts now consider ETA to be a localized terrorist organization. Autonomy and reform have removed most of its popular support. Absence of a corresponding movement in the French Basque region has kept independence an unrealized and unrealizable dream. For a small cadre of extremists, however, the struggle defines who they are, so they will continue their campaign of violence no matter how futile it has become.

Shining Path. The second case of a degenerate insurgency occurred in South America. From 1980 to 2009, Peru engaged in a bitter internal struggle, which left 70,000 dead amid widespread atrocities committed by all parties. The People's Communist Party of Peru, more commonly known as *Sendero Luminoso* (Shining Path), began in the late 1960s as a student movement led by Abimael Guzmán, who taught at the San Cristóbal of Huamanga University in the province of Ayacucho. In an environment of social inequality, labor unrest, and racial discrimination experienced by the indigenous population of the Peruvian highlands, Guzmán prepared for armed struggle, building an insurgent organization to fight the government. Shining Path adopted the Maoist model of protracted people's war, seeking to liberate rural areas out of which to expand and eventually overwhelm the cities.[77] At its peak, Shining Path had around 10,000 active members and a much larger number of supporters.[78] Guzmán declared the insurgents' goal to be "removing all the political authorities and landlords, rubbing out all functionaries. The rural areas should be thrown into confusion, the land cleansed before we sow and build up revolutionary bases of support."[79] Shining Path assassinated police, other government officials, and large landholders.

Local police lacked the resources and training to handle the deteriorating situation, so the government sent in the military. The Peruvian army made the same mistakes common to all conventional forces faced with insurgency, conducting large-scale sweeps through civilian areas. The operations netted few insurgents but produced widespread human rights abuses. Minister of War General Luís Cisnero admitted that soldiers and special police units would kill 60 people of whom perhaps three were insurgents.[80] From 1982 to 1989, the Peruvian Attorney General's Office reported 3,200 cases of "enforced disappearances," probably perpetrated by the security forces.[81] These heavy-handed tactics, combined with a draconian anti-terrorism law applied stringently to declared "emergency zones," and allegations of torture to obtain intelligence, cost the government support and benefited the insurgency, which expanded out of its base into other rural areas and into the cities of Cuzco and Lima. In the upper Huallaga Valley, the insurgents developed a patronage-client relationship with coca growers, who provided Shining Path the economic resources to expand its campaign.[82]

Fortunately for the Peruvian state, Shining Path began to lose the support of the people it purported to represent. It proved to be just as brutal as the army in forcing the peasant population to comply with its wishes. In 1989 alone, the insurgents carried out 1,298 assassinations and murdered another 1,116 "subversives."[83] Shining Path forced farmers to supply its cadres and forbade them to sell their produce to the cities. These measures significantly reduced the peasants' quality of life. In one town, insurgent measures created a food shortage that reduced average per capita consumption to one meal per day.[84] Peasants may have initially welcomed the insurgents but quickly grew to resent their oppression. Resentment prompted organized resistance as local villages, often with government help, formed civil defense committees to resist the insurgents.

Popular resistance was but one element in a series of circumstances that turned the tide of the conflict in favor of the government. In the mid-1980s, another Marxist group, Túpac Amaru, entered the struggle against the Peruvian government. Rather than work together, the two groups fought one another to the detriment of both. At the same time, the Peruvian military improved both its human rights record and its COIN tactics. British advisors helped to train the army based on the British experience in Malaya, Oman, and Northern Ireland. The government began a hearts-and-minds campaign, including a crop substitution program in the coca growing areas. The British stressed the importance of intelligence in defeating Shining Path.[85] In 1990, the government created a Special Intelligence Group.[86] The emphasis on intelligence paid a handsome dividend in 1992 with the capture of Guzmán. The police searched the trash from a suspected safe house and found skin cream used to treat psoriasis from which they knew the insurgent leader suffered. Based on this intelligence, they raided the safe house and captured Guzmán, along with several of his associates. Deprived of its charismatic leader, Shining Path began to decline. It also suffered from strategic over-reach. Success in rural areas and even in some cities led the insurgents to believe that they could move more aggressively against the government. This mistake allowed the state to use its superior resources to good effect.[87]

Having won the military struggle, however, the government of Peru failed to win the ensuing peace. Rather than consolidate its success by improving conditions in rural areas and pursuing the small remnant of the insurgency that survived, the government reverted to its policy of neglect. As a result, Shining Path has revived in a remote region of the Andes, where it has become a major coca producer. It now figures significantly in the region's thriving narcotics trade, having forged links with its Brazilian and Colombian counterparts. By 2008, the group was strong enough to attack a military convoy in the Huancavelica Region. It continues to carry out small scale attacks against police often in response to coca eradication and other anti-narcotics operations. While it seems unlikely to return to being a viable insurgency, at least in the near future, Shining Path will remain as a criminal organization for a long time to come.

The Revolutionary Armed Forces of Colombia. The Revolutionary Armed Forces of Colombia (*Fuerzas Armadas Revolucionarias de Colombia,* or FARC) was formed in the aftermath of a long period of political violence. The country's two main parties had fought a 17-year civil war, *la violencia* (1948-65), in which as many as 400,000 people died.[88] Unhappy with the peace settlement and unwilling to support either political party, Marxists formed the FARC, as well as several other insurgent groups, including the National Liberation

Army and the Popular Liberation Army; another revolutionary group, M-19, had no clear ideology.[89] Over time, the FARC emerged as the most important insurgent group.

In addition to its pervasive insurgency, Colombia also faced a serious threat from large-scale narcotics trafficking organizations. In the 1970s and 1980s, the Cali and Medellín cartels developed a near vertical monopoly on the cocaine trade, controlling coca growing and refining in Colombia and cocaine distribution throughout much of Europe, Africa, and North America. Ordinary crime, corruption, and poverty compounded the country's security problems.

The FARC established base camps in remote jungle areas and along the borders of Venezuela, Ecuador, and Panama. Those countries have proven unable or, in the case of Venezuela, unwilling to expel them. Poor peasants gave the insurgents a source of recruits and a base of support, while coca provided a ready source of cash to buy weapons. However, in the first few decades of the insurgency, narcotics-trafficking was a means to an end, not an end in itself. During the 1990s, the FARC expanded out of its rural bases to operate within Colombia's cities, including the capital of Bogota. Rural groups cooperated with urban networks and increased their revenue through extortion, kidnapping, and money laundering.[90] The conventional tactics of the Colombian armed forces proved ineffective against the insurgents. Corruption, human rights violations, and gross economic inequality exacerbated the problem.

In 1999, Colombian President Andrés Pastrana joined forces with U.S. President Bill Clinton to launch Plan Colombia, a concerted effort funded largely by the United States, to deal with narco-terrorism. Many assessments have been scathingly critical of the plan, noting its emphasis on a purely military solution and its failure to address the chronic social and economic problems that underlay both the insurgency and the narcotics trade.[91] Corruption siphoned off millions of dollars of U.S. aid and human rights abuses abounded, the dirty work farmed out by the Colombian armed forces to right-wing paramilitaries. In many respects, the Plan made a bad situation worse. Widespread fumigation of coca growing areas and sweeps by the army increased migration to the cities, swelling the ranks of the urban poor and increasing crime.

Plan Colombia actually helped the FARC by dividing the attention of the Colombian armed forces between drug cartels and insurgent groups, while failing to address the obvious connection between narcotics and insurgency. Military aid came with restrictions, allowing, for example, helicopters to be used for drug interdiction but not for COIN.[92] In fact, while it engaged the drug cartels with force, the Colombian government negotiated with the FARC. Pastrana recognized the insurgent organization as a legitimate political party and ceded them 40 percent of Colombia as a demilitarized zone in the southern part of the country. This zone provided the FARC a secure area in which it created a shadow government and a narcotics-based economy.[93]

The anti-narcotics program also contributed to the FARC's degeneration from an insurgent organization into a drug cartel by restructuring the cocaine trade. Destruction of the Cali and Medellín cartels in the 1990s and the further disruption of narcotics trafficking organizations through Plan Colombia eliminated much of the FARC's competition in the cocaine production business. By 2001, the Plan had resulted in the destruction of 818 coca base labs, the aerial spraying of 84,000 hectares of coca growing land, and the extradition of 21 drug kingpins.[94] The FARC capitalized on the disruption of traditional drug cartels by expanding its own narcotics operations. However, as the FARC transitioned to a predominantly criminal enterprise, the Colombian government intensified its campaign against the insurgents. Alvaro Uribe Velez won the 2002 presidential election, promising to deal with the FARC, whose unwillingness to negotiate in good faith strengthened popular support for a purely military solution to the insurgency.[95] True to his word, Uribe launched a sustained offensive against the insurgents. At the same time, he disarmed right-wing militaries, increasing the legitimacy of his own armed forces. This military campaign achieved striking results. From 2003 to 2009, the Colombian military claimed to have killed 10,806 members of the FARC and captured 26,648; another 11,615 demobilized of their own accord.[96] Estimates of current FARC membership range from 7,000-10,000, half of its peak strength of 17-20,000 in 2000.[97]

Despite these heavy losses, the FARC has proven remarkably resilient. It has coped with the new situation by decentralizing its command and control, abandoning large-scale operations for guerrilla tactics, making excellent use of land mines, and rebuilding its base of support in remote areas among indigenous people.[98] In the process of adapting to a less friendly security environment, however, the FARC has become less like a revolutionary insurgency and more like a narcotics cartel, or perhaps like a series of smaller criminal outfits. It is a major player in the cocaine industry, thanks to the restructuring of the drug trade inadvertently caused by the U.S.-backed drug war.

This effort destroyed the cartels, which had enjoyed a vertical monopoly of the cocaine trade from production through distribution. They have been replaced by a series of smaller groups controlling various aspects of the process. The Mexican criminal organizations have benefited from the disruption of Caribbean trade routes, gaining control of land smuggling through Central America and building a vast distribution network in the United States.[99]The FARC, which had previously taxed coca growing and processing, now controls these stages directly.[100] The role of middlemen in the operation, those refining the coca paste and feeding it into the Mexican distribution system, has been taken over by 200-400 "new illegal armed groups" or "baby cartels."[101]

The Colombian government has reduced the FARC's strength, perhaps even to the point where it no longer threatens survival of the Colombian state. However, the insurgents have carved out a living space in which they exercise shadow governance. Dislodging them from that niche has proven very difficult. FARC groups continue to be well armed, organized and funded by drug money. Barring some significant change in these circumstances, they are likely to remain a permanent fixture in the Colombian underworld, along with a host of other nefarious groups.

Why Insurgencies Degenerate. Insurgencies have a shelf life. They succeed, fail, or degenerate into mere terrorism or criminality. In most cases, this degeneration occurs when the government wins the military struggle but fails to win the peace that follows. If insurgents are not reintegrated into legitimate society and politics, they will continue the struggle in the hope (however forlorn) of one day restoring their fortunes and winning the war. In those cases in which the criminal activity that once funded the insurgency proves extremely lucrative, they may engage in criminality as an end in itself.

Group 4: Success Through Co-Option.

Understanding how and why insurgencies degenerate suggests a strategy for resolving them more effectively. Insurgencies that cannot be decisively defeated by a traditional COIN strategy may be resolved through co-option. A threatened government must fight the insurgents to a standstill and then find a way to draw them into the legitimate political process. Three campaigns commend themselves as useful examples of victory achieved through co-option: Northern Ireland (1969-2005), El Salvador (1979-92), and Sierra Leone (1991-2002).

Northern Ireland. The longest insurgency Britain has ever faced began innocently enough as a civil rights movement. Northern Ireland remained part of the UK when the rest of Ireland gained independence in 1921. The Province's Protestant majority systematically subjugated the Catholic population through institutionalized discrimination and the use of draconian emergency laws. Gerrymandered election districts kept Catholics under-represented, even on the councils of local communities in which they were the majority. Protestants received a disproportionate share of public housing, and Catholic unemployment exceeded Protestant by a factor of 2.62 to 1 in 1971.[102] To enforce this system of apartheid, the authorities made extensive use of the 1922 Civil Authorities (Special Powers) Act, which gave them extraordinary powers of arrest and detention without trial. The almost exclusively Protestant Royal Ulster Constabulary (RUC), the UK's only armed police force, could call upon its paramilitary reservists the "B Specials" to handle unrest.

Inspired by the nonviolent civil rights movement in the United States, Catholic students at Queens University, Belfast, created the Northern Ireland Civil Rights Association and began demonstrating to protest discrimination. Their protests turned violent during the summer of 1969, when demonstrators clashed with members of Protestant Orange Lodges during marches to commemorate the 1689 siege of Derry. Rioting spread throughout the province, and on August 14, the hard-pressed police asked London for troops. What began as a temporary deployment soon turned into a COIN campaign that would last almost 40 years.

Despite having more COIN experience than any other army in the world, the British spent 3 years of trial and error, making many mistakes that would hamper their effort for the remainder of the conflict. Many of these errors arose, however, because the troops operated in support of a provincial government that used them to defend the Protestant ascendency. The government in Westminster compounded the problem by declaring Catholic neighborhoods in Belfast and Londonderry "no-go areas," pulling back the army and police in hopes that doing so would quell unrest. This strategy had exactly the opposite effect. The Provisional Irish Republican Army (PIRA), which split from the main organization that had fought for Irish independence in 1919-21, moved in to fill the void, transforming the civil rights movement into an armed struggle to expel the British and unite Northern Ireland with the Irish Republic. PIRA grew dramatically, increasing from 100 members in January 1970 to 800 by December, and began to attack the army and police with sniping and bombs.[103] The insurgents enjoyed widespread support among Catholics. The number of active fighters at any given moment arose from a strategic decision on optimal deployment rather than from lack of volunteers. PIRA also had a safe haven across the border in the Irish Republic. The conflict continued to escalate as security force actions made a bad situation worse. The army conducted massive searches in the Lower Falls Roads area of Belfast, turning a "sullen Catholic population into a downright hostile one."[104] Large-scale internment of Catholic suspects, most of whom were innocent, further alienated the population, as did "interrogation in depth," the controversial tactics (hooding, wall standing, sleep deprivation, etc.) that have caused so much controversy at Abu Ghraib and Guantanamo Bay. The downward spiral culminated in the January 1972 incident known as Bloody Sunday in which British paratroopers opened fire on demonstrators in Derry, killing 13.

By the end of 1972, the conflict had settled into a familiar pattern. The security forces hunkered down for a long struggle, and PIRA reorganized itself into a hub-and-spoke cell system, whose hub (the "general staff") resided safely across the border in the Irish Republic. Tit-for-tat killings took the lives of numerous Catholics and Protestants, as PIRA and Protestant paramilitaries such as the Ulster Defense Association murdered ordinary Catholics and Protestants. The British military deployed its elite Special Forces unit, the Special Air Service (SAS), to support its 12 infantry battalions and the RUC. The SAS soon became embroiled in controversial killings, which added more fuel to the flames of unrest. For its part, PIRA began bombing targets in England. Meanwhile, the insurgents received financial support from the Irish-

American community and weapons from the government of Libya, which also allowed PIRA to train on its territory.

Meanwhile, the British government undertook much needed political and social reform in the province. It began by revoking provincial autonomy, ruling Northern Ireland directly from Westminster. London poured billions of pounds sterling into improving living conditions in Catholic neighborhoods in hopes of undermining support for the insurgents. By 1992, the Northern Ireland Housing Authority had built 17,000 new homes in Belfast and another 1,800 in Londonderry.[105] The differential in unemployment, especially in the public sector, improved somewhat after the British passed strong anti-discrimination legislation. Equality had hardly been achieved, but living conditions for Catholics improved significantly.

The summer of 1989 saw the 20th anniversary of what both sides refer to as "the Troubles." Two decades of fighting had produced a military stalemate. The British Army could not destroy the PIRA, but the PIRA could do little more than persist in its desultory struggle.[106] It had failed to accomplish the one thing essential to victory: persuading the British public that the cost of retaining Northern Ireland had become too high. The conflict had not been an issue in any of the British General Elections since 1969. Under such circumstances, stalemate worked against the insurgents as ordinary Catholics and Protestants grew weary of the incessant conflict. Under such circumstances, the door for a negotiated settlement opened wide. As historian Richard English concludes, the insurgents realized that "their own violence was going neither to win the war, nor to improve upon a bargaining position that offered both definite results and the prospect of increasing rewards achieved through political process."[107]

Washington and Dublin supported peace talks, as did London. However, because Conservative Prime Minister John Major depended on 12 Protestant Members of Parliament from Northern Ireland to maintain his slim majority, he had limited negotiating room. Major did achieve a temporary ceasefire in 1994, but a peace accord would have to await the Labour Party's 1997 landslide victory. Tony Blair achieved what none of his predecessors could, a lasting peace leading to a power-sharing agreement that brought insurgent leaders into a Northern Ireland government via their political party, Sinn Fein. The Good Friday Accords signed in 1998 provided both immediate peace and a continuing peace process that would bear fruit over the next decade, thanks in no small measure to the 9/11 attacks, which discredited all forms of terrorism. It was no accident that Jerry Adams announced decommissioning of PIRA's weapons right after al-Qaeda's July 2005 bombing of the London Underground. The power-sharing executive still does not function very well, but renewal of the insurgency seems unlikely. Ordinary Catholic men and women are heartily sick of war.

El Salvador. The Salvadoran civil war (1979-92) provides another good example of how to resolve an insurgency through a combination of military force, political reform, and diplomacy, all supported by an outside power (the United States). However, none of the parties to the conflict anticipated or wanted such an outcome. The insurgents were determined to overthrow a corrupt and brutal regime that was equally determined to crush them. The United States, under the leadership of its staunchly anti-communist President Ronald Reagan, paid lip service to human rights but was far more interested in defeating the Marxist revolutionaries. Only the confluence of fortuitous circumstances and a change in the U.S. approach, perhaps brought on by the election of George H. W. Bush and the end of the Cold War, made possible success through co-option, a resolution to the conflict by drawing the insurgents into the legitimate political process within a reformed state.

In 1979, El Salvador was one of the poorest countries in Latin America and one of the most undemocratic. Fifteen families controlled an economy in which 1 percent of the population (approximately 4.7 million) owned 70 percent of the land.[108] The military routinely intervened to prevent reform, suppress rebellion, and support the oligarchs. When the army blocked land reform in 1979, opposition turned violent. In 1980, various resistance groups united to form the *Farabundo Marti National Liberation Front* (FMLN), named for a Communist Labor leader and organizer. The movement enjoyed considerable support among the country's rural peasants and urban poor, which increased as the army and paramilitary death squads (composed of off-duty soldiers) conducted reprisals against those even suspected of supporting the insurgents. The FMLN fielded 12,000 fighters supported by a much larger group of noncombatants.[109]

From 1980 to 1983, the insurgents had the upper hand against a conventional army filled with demoralized conscripts. The FMLN enjoyed support from Cuba, the new Communist Sandinista government in Nicaragua, and, indirectly through these intermediaries, from the Soviet Union. They had safe havens in remote border areas of Honduras and Guatemala. The insurgents became strong enough to overrun the Air

Force's main airbase, destroying most of its aircraft on the ground, which enabled them to operate in large columns and engage substantial army formations. As large areas of the country fell under FMLN control, U.S. military advisors warned that, without substantial support, the Salvadoran government would lose the war.[110]

The Reagan administration responded with a massive infusion of economic and military aid. However, the experience of Vietnam was too fresh for the American public to sanction direct intervention by U.S. forces. The new approach to COIN, known as the Nixon Doctrine, promised "foreign aid for internal defense," including deployment of small Special Forces teams to advise and train the host nation's military. However, the horrible human rights record of the Salvadoran armed forces made it difficult for the United States to justify even this limited assistance. In the most infamous incident, the American-trained Atlacatl battalion massacred almost the entire village of El Mazote in December 1981. All told, the security forces murdered approximately 50,000 unarmed civilians, most during the early 1980s.[111]

The Reagan administration did, of course, care about human rights, but not as much as it cared about fighting communism. The Salvadoran military correctly deduced that the United States would not make aide contingent upon improving its human rights record, so it resisted pressure to do so. Equipment, training, and money allowed the military to stem but not reverse the FMLN tide. Airplanes and helicopters forced the insurgents to rely less on large-scale operations in favor of traditional guerrilla tactics and to concentrate on attacking economic targets rather than the Salvadoran army.[112] However, it still retained the ability to mount a major operation. In November 1989, the FMLN launched an offensive against the capital San Salvador, occupying some of its wealthiest neighborhoods. While the offensive did not threaten the survival of the state, it made a mockery of Salvadoran military claims that the FMLN would soon be defeated. To make matters worse, members of the army murdered six Jesuit priests, along with the wife and daughter of a custodian at the University of the Americas. The FMLN and the Salvadoran armed forces had reached a stalemate.

This stalemate, along with drastically altered political circumstances, made both parties amenable to a negotiated settlement. The fall of the Berlin Wall lead to diminished support for both parties to the conflict.[113]The government and the insurgents both moderated their demands. The FMLN backed off its insistence on power sharing and much of its social agenda, while the government proved amenable to reducing the size, power, and influence of the army. A ceasefire followed by almost 2 years of negotiations under the auspices of the UN facilitated by the United States led to the signing of peace accords in January 1991.

The accords began by restructuring the security sector. The army would be reduced by 50 percent (by 1993) and confined to defending national sovereignty from external threats. The National Guard, Treasury Police, and National Police, which had been under military control, would also be disbanded and replaced with a new civilian police force. Some former FMLN guerrillas were integrated into the new police force; the rest were demobilized. The accords called for a National Restructuring Plan, which provided land grants to 47,500 veterans from both the

Salvadoran Armed Forces and the FMLN.[114] The constitution was amended to expand the electorate and institute other reforms. As a result, the FMLN became the second party of the country. On March 15, 2009, its candidate, Mauricio Funes, became President of El Salvador. Despite this electoral victory by the former insurgents, El Salvador remains a U.S. ally.

While the American intervention in El Salvador can hardly be called an unqualified success, it nonetheless provides useful lessons for resolving insurgencies. The conflict killed 75,000 of El Salvador's 5.3 million people (1990), most of them innocent civilians. The United States invested $3.2 billion in economic and $1.1 billion in military aide trying to destroy the FMLN.[115] Only when military victory seemed improbable, and in the face of vastly altered circumstances, did it settle for the second-best solution of a negotiated settlement. El Salvador remains an impoverished country with a grossly inequitable distribution of wealth. However, current economic conditions and the cost of the conflict in blood and treasure aside, the accords have produced a remarkably durable peace. Both parties have seen that they can accomplish their goals through a political process that has a high degree of integrity. The case of El Salvador suggests that sometimes the best outcome to a conflict is one in which both sides believe they have won. Had the United States pursued such a compromise solution from the outset, the same result might have been accomplished with far less bloodshed.

Sierra Leone. The tiny West African nation of Sierra Leone provides the third example of insurgency resolved through co-option. When it received independence from the British in 1961, the country possessed a decent infrastructure, a trained professional civil service, and a lucrative resource—diamonds. However, deep ethnic divisions and a culture of corruption eroded these advantages. Poverty, inequitable distribution of wealth, and political repression fueled unrest.

In 1991, the country had a population of 4.27 million, 99 percent of them Africans belonging to 13 different tribes. Per capita annual income was $325, literacy 21 percent, and life expectancy was 42 years.[116] For 6 years, the Sierra Leone People's Party (SLPP) governed the country. In 1967, the All People's Party (APP) narrowly won elections, and Siaka Stevens became prime minister. Three military coups, based in part on tribal considerations, rocked the country over the next year. After the restoration of order, Stevens resumed his office and in 1971 transformed Sierra Leone from a parliamentary democracy to a republic with himself as President, an office he would hold until 1985. In 1978, he amended the constitution and made the country a one-party state.

Although Stevens sowed the seeds of insurgency, his hand-picked successor, Joseph Momoh, would reap them. Under mounting international pressure, Momoh set up a constitutional review committee to consider political problems, but he had little incentive to restore real democracy. Revolution offered the only alternative to continued one-party rule. In 1991, a group of students and other dissidents led by Foday Sanko formed the Revolutionary United Front (RUF) and launched an insurgency against the Momoh government. RUF operated from safe havens in neighboring Liberia, also in a state of civil war, and enjoyed the support of Liberian strongman Charles Taylor, as well as the assistance of mercenaries from neighboring

Burkina Faso.[117] The RUF soon gained control of some of the country's diamond mines, giving the insurgents a lucrative source of revenue to buy weapons and support its operations. Because "blood diamonds" could not be sold on the open market, the insurgents laundered their rough diamonds through Ivory Coast and other willing neighbors.[118]

The success of RUF put Sierra Leone on a roller coaster of violence inflicted first by the insurgents, then by the government. Momoh was replaced by a coup and fled the country. The new government could not halt the advance of RUF, which by 1995 was poised to overrun the capital of Freetown. To prevent the defeat, the military leadership hired mercenaries from the South African company Executive Outcomes (EO), who helped stem the RUF tide. Free elections in 1996 led to a ceasefire, which collapsed after yet another coup. The following year, troops of the Economic Organization of West African States Monitoring Group (ECOMOG) restored civilian government and enforced a ceasefire. Peace Accords were signed in 1999, to be implemented by a UN mission with 6,000 troops, and RUF joined a coalition government. However, peace ended with the withdrawal of ECOMOG troops in April 2000. In May, violence broke out in the capital. The UK sent troops to evacuate British subjects and restore order. A new ceasefire held. Elections in 2002 saw the SLPP win a decisive victory, while RUF failed to gain a single seat. From 2002 to 2006, the British and UN gradually withdrew their troops as rebel forces demobilized. The peace has held, thanks in no small measure to the United States ending the civil war in neighboring Liberia.

As in the cases of El Salvador and Northern Ireland, resolution of the conflict came as a result of military stalemate. Without external support from EO, ECOMOG, the British Army, and the UN, the insurgents would have won. However, while each of those forces restored civilian rule, none of them was willing and/or able to destroy the RUF. By staying long enough to maintain order, though, the UN and the British convinced the insurgents that they could not win in the foreseeable future. The end of the Liberian civil war and mounting international pressure made it clear to the RUF that they could accomplish little by continuing the armed struggle. These circumstances paved the way for a viable peace through a process of demobilizing and reintegrating insurgent fighters into civil society, while including their political wing in legitimate politics.

The 1999 Lomé Peace Accords created the framework for conflict resolution, though a lasting ceasefire did not occur until 2002. The accords granted an amnesty for combatants and provided for "transformation of the RUF/SL [Sierra Leone] into a political party," participating in a coalition government. The Accord also dealt with security, allowing former insurgents to join Sierra Leona's new armed forces "provided they meet established criteria" for doing so. The new armed forces would also reflect the ethnic makeup of the nation as would the legislature, which had seats designated for tribal chiefdoms. Those insurgents who did not serve in the new armed forces would be cantoned, demobilized, and reintegrated into society in a manner to be determined and with outside financial support.[119]

The UN Mission in Sierra Leone (UNAMSIL) oversaw implementation of the peace accords. In 2003, it reported that, although the security situation was stable, border areas remained a problem, especially the

Liberian border because of the civil war in that country.[120] Two years later, the situation had improved considerably with the end of the Liberian conflict. The biggest security problems were delay in implementing reintegration programs for former fighters due to lack of funds and high unemployment, especially among young people.[121] UNAMSIL came to an end 6 months later. By the fall of 2010, the situation had improved so much that the new UN Peace Building Commission focused on ordinary crime, corruption, and narcotics trafficking rather than political violence as the most serious security problems.[122]

The sad episode of Sierra Leone is hardly one of which the international community can be proud. Only after the country had become a virtual failed state did the UK and the UN intervene. Nonetheless, they successfully resolved the conflict through a combination of co-option and development. ECOMOG, and later the British, fought the insurgents to a stalemate, creating circumstances for a negotiated peace accord, whose implementation was overseen by the UN. Economic and social development continues, albeit at a slow pace, but renewed civil war seems unlikely for the foreseeable future. Had it not been for international intervention to force a negotiated settlement, RUF might have become like FARC, a criminal enterprise controlling Sierra Leone's lucrative diamond trade.

Winning through Co-option. The three cases examined suggest that the best resolution for insurgency is one that allows both sides to believe they have won. Living conditions for Catholics in Northern Ireland have improved dramatically, and the institutions of government, especially law enforcement and justice, function more equitably that at any time since partition. Power-sharing remains problematic, but neither side wishes to resume violent conflict. The FMLN succeeded in making El Salvador a functioning democracy, even if they fell far short of achieving a just economic order. Development in Sierra Leone continues slowly, but the political system has been reformed to accommodate ethnic divisions that contributed to the outbreak of civil war.

LESSONS

The four groups of insurgencies examined in this monograph yield definite lessons that may inform not only the conduct of COIN campaigns by the U.S. Army, but the larger political question of what American intervention to support a threatened state can realistically accomplish. To being with, the six campaigns in Groups 1 and 2 clearly indicate that only under very unusual circumstances do insurgencies end in clear cut victory for one side or the other. Insurgents may win *if* the government they oppose enjoys little support or even tolerance by its own people, *if* they have a source of supply and a safe haven across a friendly border and/or external support, and *if* the threatened government is not supported by a friendly power that considers the cost in blood and treasure of a protracted intervention worthwhile. With few exceptions, such favorable circumstances occurred only during the 20-year period of decolonization following World War II.

Complete government victories have been almost as rare as insurgent triumphs. A threatened government can win *if* it can address the root causes of social and economic unrest on which the insurgency feeds *while* isolating the insurgents from outside support, and *provided* it enjoys support from a friendly power, or at least the acquiescence of the international community as it suppresses the insurgents. The British victory over Malayan Communists occurred on a peninsula with a virtually impenetrable northern border, defeat of LTTE occurred on an island, and the U.S.-backed Greek government won after Yugoslavia closed its border and isolated the insurgents.

Unfortunately, the examples in Group 3 represent a large and growing category of degenerate insurgencies that plague the world today. The longer a conflict drags on, the more likely that the insurgents will degenerate into mere terrorists, capable of carrying out limited attacks but of doing nothing else, or that the insurgent organization will transform itself into a criminal enterprise with or without the ideological cover of legitimate revolution. Groups like ETA that degenerate into small terrorist organizations can probably be eliminated or reduced to insignificance over time as popular support for them wanes if the government considers it cost-effective to destroy rather than just contain them. Insurgencies that become criminal enterprises are far more problematic, especially if they have access to a lucrative resource like narcotics. The Colombian government has reduced the FARC's strength and constrained its operating space to the point where it no longer threatens survival of the state. In the process, it has inadvertently aided the group's transition to a criminal enterprise. Shining Path has undergone a similar transition owing to failure of the Peruvian state to consolidate its success in the 1990s through economic and social development in the areas in which the insurgency enjoyed support.

The best way to prevent insurgencies degenerating into chronic problems is to resolve them before they reach that point. The cases in Group 4 suggest the most promising approach to achieving such resolution. In each case, the threatened government settled on a strategy of co-option only after prolonged efforts to defeat the insurgents failed. Only when they reached military stalemate, a situation in which both sides realized that they could not decisively win a military contest, did the belligerents resolve their conflict through negotiation and compromise. Achieving such a stalemate is costly in blood and treasure. However, had co-option been the goal from the outset, the same result might have been achieved earlier with less loss of life. On the other hand, PIRA, the FMLN, and RUF had to be convinced that they could achieve little by continuing armed struggle before they would negotiate in good faith. Thus, while the period of military conflict may be shortened, it probably cannot be eliminated. The insurgents must be fought to a stalemate.

In each Group 4 case, intervention by an outside power proved crucial to resolving the insurgency. Northern Ireland is, of course, part of the UK, but the government in London behaved much like an intervening power in the province. Certainly the Catholic population and even many Protestants perceived it as a foreign entity. By 1998, however, London had come to be seen less as an occupier and more as an honest broker. Its position on Northern Ireland was clear. Any change in the political status of the province required approval of the majority of Northern Irish men and women. Until then, it must be governed fairly through some sort of power-sharing arrangement. In El Salvador, the United States provided the military and economic aid necessary for the Salvadoran government to fend off the FMLN. After the 1989 insurgent offensive, the United States pushed its ally to the negotiating table, making aid contingent upon reform and an improved human rights record. In Sierra Leone, EO, ECOMOG, Britain, and the UN intervened to prevent RUF from seizing power. However, none of these entities could or would engage in a protracted campaign to defeat the insurgents completely. Intervention combined with growing international pressure on the blood diamond trade may have prevented RUF from becoming an African FARC. At the end of the day, it had more to gain from negotiations than it did from continued violence. In each of these cases, the intervening power(s) also remained engaged after peace accords had been signed, providing advice and material assistance during the delicate process of demobilization and reintegration of combatants.

A STRATEGY OF CO-OPTION

The U.S. Army's strategic thinking on COIN should be based upon two premises. First, during the foreseeable future, the Army's only COIN role will be to support a threatened state. Second, based upon the preceding analysis of past campaigns, insurgencies can best be brought to a successful conclusion through a strategy of co-option. While it involves the use of military force, such a strategy is first and foremost political. The following broad recommendations might provide guidance in developing a strategy of co-option:

1. *Develop a Comprehensive Strategy Before Deploying.* Any time American forces deploy to invade a country or act in support of a threatened state, policymakers should devise a comprehensive strategy for all contingencies, including a protracted COIN campaign and/or a significant nation building effort. This strategy should integrate diplomatic, informational, military, economic, financial, intelligence, and law enforcement

components into a unified political strategy rather than treating nonmilitary elements as ancillary to a predominantly military campaign. The wars in Afghanistan and Iraq have been more costly in lives and treasure than they might have been had policymakers developed a contingency plan for a protracted COIN campaign before the conflicts began.

Several Army officers and some policymakers pushed for such a plan in the immediate aftermath of the invasion, but the Pentagon blocked their efforts, wishing to withdraw troops as soon as possible. Richard Haass, who served as the Bush administration's coordinator for the future of Afghanistan, wanted a post conflict stability operation. "I pressed for a U.S. military presence of some 25,000–30,000 troops (matched by an equal number from NATO countries)," he reported. These troops would have been "part of an international force that would help maintain order after the invasion and train Afghans until they could protect themselves." His suggestion got a cool reception. "My colleagues in the Bush administration had no interest in my proposal." [123] Administration policymakers had the same reaction to suggestions about a follow-on mission in Iraq. As early as March 19, 2003, the Special Operations Force staff officer working on Phase IV (post-conflict) plans urged preparation for a protracted COIN campaign. He was explicitly told not even to mention the word "counterinsurgency." [124]

2. *Intervene sooner rather than later.* Insurgencies are like fires. The sooner they are spotted, the easier they are to put out. Governments have been slow to recognize and respond to insurgent threats and even slower to request outside help. Delay gives insurgents time to widen their base of support among a disaffected

population. COIN requires not only a timely response but an appropriate one, a response that does not over-rely on conventional military means, which usually make a bad situation worse. Since governments, like individuals, have a hard time recognizing their own problems, a supporting nation like the United States should advise its allies about the internal threats it recognizes and encourage them to ask for help in a timely manner.

3. *Steepen the Learning Curve.* Almost every COIN campaign begins with a period of trial and error as conventional armed forces adjust to unconventional war. Even when the military in question has had extensive COIN experience, a period of adjustment still occurs. Despite half a century of imperial policing and COIN, the British army took about 3 years to get it right in Northern Ireland, the same amount of time the United States needed to develop an appropriate strategy for Iraq. While some period of adjustment is probably inevitable, it need not be as long as it has been to date. By preserving both contemporary experience and the learning institutions that teach it to new recruits, such as the Human Terrain Mapping System, the Leadership Development and Education Program, and other such education and training programs, the U.S. Army can steepen the learning curve for future campaigns and reduce the adjustment period.

4. *Keep the U.S. Foot Print as Small as Possible.* The larger the U.S. force deployed to aide a threatened ally and the longer it remains, the more it will look like an army of occupation. Under such circumstances, the insurgents may then be able to transform the conflict into a nationalist struggle against the hated foreigner,

winning even more support for their cause. U.S. advisers and supporting forces must make the host nation fight its own war. Keeping the American or coalition presence as small as possible is the best way to accomplish this goal. A handful of advisers in El Salvador accomplished a great deal, especially during the last phase of the war. The doctrinal guidance under which they operate still has much to commend it today. *Field Manual (FM) 100-20, Military Operations in Low-Intensity Conflict* (1990) warned that deploying too many U.S. troops would "Americanize" the conflict, "destroying the legitimacy of the entity [the threatened government] we are attempting to assist."[125]

5. *Make U.S. Aide Contingent upon Political Reform and Regard for Human Rights*. A threatened government that refuses to become more responsive to the needs of its own people deserves to lose. The highly desirable outcome of the Salvadoran Civil War might have been achieved sooner and with far less loss of life had the Reagan administration taken the same approach as its successor. The real threat of a reduction or cut off of U.S. aid encouraged the Salvadoran government to negotiate with the FMLN. The inability or perhaps unwillingness of the United States and its allies to pressure the Karzai government to reduce corruption sufficiently to regain its legitimacy is seriously undermining the COIN effort in Afghanistan.

However, making aid contingent upon reform is much easier said than done. If a threatened government realizes its importance to the United States, it can resist pressure, knowing it will still get aid. The Salvadoran government understood this fact as does the Karzai regime. Reforming in the middle of a conflict may also make a government more vulnerable to subversion. Under such circumstances, a willingness to engage in political reform and a long-term plan for doing so, coupled with some highly visible first steps, may be the most that can be done in a crisis. It is also important to remember that "reform" does not mean creating a Western-style democracy, but rather increasing the legitimacy of a government in the eyes of its own people based upon their needs and expectations. A demonstrated willingness to compromise and to negotiate with insurgents is, however, crucial to the success of a co-option strategy.

While engaging in political reform is a tortuous process that takes time, avoiding human rights violations can and must be done immediately. The correlation between repression and government defeat is very high.[126] Indiscriminate use of force against innocent civilians, torture of suspects to gather intelligence, and other human rights violations undermine government legitimacy and usually lead to defeat. The communications revolution has made every person with a cell phone a potential reporter and increased transparency to such a degree that knowledge of abuses rapidly becomes public.

6. *Harmonize COIN and Anti-Crime Efforts.* Insurgencies develop in an environment of weak governance. In such an environment, much of the economy is grey or black, and organized crime often thrives. A government threatened by insurgency usually faces significant criminality as well. Given the nexus that often develops between these two threats, a strategy to fight one must also tackle the other. Focusing on COIN while ignoring organized crime (or vice versa) may have the undesirable effect of diminishing the one

problem while exacerbating the other. Insurgents may join criminal enterprises and/or insurgent groups may become criminal organizations themselves.

The link between insurgency, organized crime, and narcotics trafficking is particularly problematic. FARC and Shining Path funded their insurgencies with money from the cocaine trade. Both have transformed themselves into criminal enterprises. Opium production funds the Taliban and al-Qaeda; enriches members of the Afghan government, including President Karzai's own brother; and provides a subsistence living for many poor farmers. Eradication efforts have focused on the farmers, who make little money and are often forced by the Taliban to grow poppies. Depriving these farmers of their cash crop without giving them an alternative and providing them the security in which to grow it helps the insurgents, not the government.

7. *Win the Peace*. Every time U.S. forces deploy, the American public asks, "When will the troops come home?" Political discourse around missions often reduces to a single, most unhelpful question: "Should we stay or should we leave?" The answer is "neither," if staying means becoming a permanent occupier and leaving means withdrawing all U.S. forces by a fixed, pre-determined date. The key to successful COIN lies in remaining engaged with the threatened government in the appropriate way for each stage of the protracted conflict. The period after the end of hostilities is crucial. Shining Path has revived in Peru because the Peruvian government failed to consolidate its success against the insurgent organization with economic and social development in the areas where the insurgents enjoyed popular support. The Iraqi insurgency broke

out largely because the United States lacked the troop strength and the determination to maintain law and order, and did not have a viable reconstruction plan following the fall of Baghdad. Better planning and preparation might have prevented the looting and concomitant damage to infrastructure that occurred, and perhaps the insurgency would never have gotten off the ground. At the very least, the lawlessness would have been less widespread.

The U.S. Army does not, of course, get to pick its wars, and so it cannot insist that the above conditions be met before it deploys. For example, U.S. advisors understood the importance of respecting human rights in winning the Salvadoran conflict, but they were powerless to pressure Salvadoran officers who knew that Washington cared more about fighting Communism than it did about preventing abuses. To reaffirm an often quoted but frequently ignored truism of Clausewitz, "war is an instrument of policy," and policy is made by civilians. Civilian politicians must answer to voters impatient for results. Only when the very survival of the nation is at stake will the American people support substantial expenditures in blood and treasure over an extended period of time. Intervening to support an ally threatened by insurgency is rarely a popular mission.

While the military does not (and should not) make policy, military officers are frequently asked their views on policy issues. At such times, they can and must raise the difficult concerns discussed in this analysis. Foremost among these concerns should be the question of whether the U.S. Government can sustain political will for a protracted COIN campaign abroad, a question that must be asked before it deploys U.S.

forces. If it does not seem likely that political will can be sustained, the intervention should be seriously reconsidered.

IMPLICATIONS FOR IRAQ AND AFGHANISTAN

An analysis of this nature would be incomplete without consideration of its implications for the current conflicts in Iraq and Afghanistan. These wars have been underway for 7 and 9 years respectively, and it is, of course, neither possible to correct mistakes made early in each nor to foresee precisely how each will end. Nonetheless, the conclusions herein do allow for assessment of the U.S. effort to date in each case and for commentary on the direction each mission seems to be heading. The assessment bodes well for the Iraq mission but raises serious concerns about operations in Afghanistan.

For its first 3 years in Iraq, the United States made every mistake that can be made in an unconventional operation. To begin with, American forces entered Baghdad without a plan to conduct a protracted COIN campaign. In the aftermath of Vietnam, the Army had subsumed COIN into broad task groups such as "Low-Intensity Conflict," "Operations Other than War," and "Stability and Support Operations," catch-all categories for missions that it did not want to perform and preferred to relegate to Special Forces. This decision left the vast majority of the regular forces unprepared for a protracted COIN campaign. While several military manuals published after Vietnam reveal this dislike of unconventional conflict, two in particular illustrate the limited role the U.S. military expected to play in COIN.[127] *FM 100-20: Military Opera-*

tions in Low-Intensity Conflict (1990) asserted that "U.S military support to insurgencies . . . will normally center on security assistance program administration efforts that complement those of other U.S. Government agencies."[128]*Joint Publication (JP) 3-07: Doctrine for Joint Operations in Low-Intensity Conflict* echoed this theme, asserting that U.S. support for COIN would usually be limited to "furnishing suitable material, training, services, and advisors."[129]

While lack of training for and experience with COIN hurt the campaign, the overwhelming failure lay in the realm of political strategy. The Bush administration deployed too few troops for the task at hand. Many senior officers, including Army Chief of Staff General Eric Shinseki and the former Central Command Commander General (retired) Anthony Zinni had argued for a more robust invasion force with a follow-on peace and stability mission. However, Secretary of Defense Donald Rumsfeld ignored this advice on the size of the invasion force and dismissed the need for a post-conflict stability operation. As a result, the Army and Marines invaded with more than enough troops to defeat the Iraqi armed forces but far too few to occupy and maintain order in a country more than twice the size of Idaho, with 26 million people. The troops they did have lacked the training, equipment, and experience for an internal security operation, which the administration had determined beforehand not to perform. Many observers complained that the Pentagon "seemed to be more concerned with persuading the U.S. electorate that invading Iraq would not lead to a Vietnam-style quagmire than it was with the vagaries of post-war nation building."[130]

The conflict took a turn for the better with a change of course in 2007. In late 2006, a bipartisan Study

Group warned that the situation in Iraq was deteriorating.[131] Contrary to popular belief, the new "surge" strategy adopted by the coalition involved much more than the deployment of 20,000 to 30,000 additional U.S. troops. Under General David Petraeus, the United States took greater advantage of the "Anbar Awakening," a spontaneous, ad hoc movement among Sunni Iraqis in Anbar province. The Awakening began in 2005 when leaders from the Abu Mahal tribe approached the Americans, asking for help to fight al-Qaeda in Iraq, which threatened their historic position in Anbar. Petraeus recognized that since both the Americans and the Iraqis hated the foreign mujahedeen, he could make strategic use of this grassroots movement, which by the end of 2007 numbered 65,000 to 80,000 (many of them former insurgents). Concerned Local Citizens Councils (CLCs) facilitated cooperation between the Sunni Tribes and coalition forces.[132] Supported by funds from the Commanders Emergency Response Program, CLCs produced the kind of cooperation that yielded good intelligence so that the military could use force in a focused, effective manner with minimal collateral damage.[133] This willingness to work with local Iraqis, including former insurgents, has been very effective. Along with improved programs to train Iraqi soldiers and police, the new strategy allowed the United States to reduce its troop strength to 55,000 during the summer of 2010.

The new U.S. COIN approach is exactly the sort of co-option strategy, albeit on a much larger scale, that worked in Northern Ireland, El Salvador, and Sierra Leone. The United States began as an occupation force but gradually transitioned to the role of a supporting power. In that role, it has pushed for reintegration of former insurgents into legitimate politics and social life. Despite sporadic intercommunal violence, Iraq continues on a path towards peace and stability. The United States will need to remain engaged with and supportive of the Iraqi government for years to come, but there is every reason to believe that doing so will produce the desired result: an independent, democratic and stable Iraq capable of defending itself from internal and external threats.

The situation in Afghanistan is far less encouraging. The war unfolded in a very different manner than the invasion of Iraq and under circumstances far less favorable to establishing peace and stability. The United States also missed a window of opportunity to defeat the insurgents decisively, a window which may not open again. A U.S.-backed offensive by the Northern Alliance of non-Pashtun tribes toppled the hated Taliban regime and installed the government of Hamid Karzai. However, the Bush administration had no interest in a protracted nation-building mission. Instead of aggressively pursuing the Taliban and al-Qaeda following Operation ANACONDA (March 2002), it handed over security responsibility to NATO's International Stabilization Force (ISAF), refused to commit a larger U.S. presence, and prepared to invade Iraq. The UN and a host of nongovernmental, international, and private volunteer organizations descended on Afghanistan to engage in development and capacity building.

ISAF and its civilian counterparts not only failed to improve significantly security and living conditions for ordinary Afghans, but they may have made the situation worse. "The International Community's lukewarm response to Afghanistan after 9/11," declared one regional expert, "has been matched only by its incompetence, incoherence, and conflicting strategies."[134] This statement may be overly harsh, but it does correctly identify lack of a unified effort among the myriad nations, agencies, and organizations as an impediment to success of the polyglot mission. The Rumsfeld Pentagon also applied the wrong approach to internal security. For 6 years, the United States treated the Taliban as "mere terrorists," a threat that could be countered by killing or capturing key leaders in each group. Only in 2007 did the Pentagon begin to appreciate what units on the ground had known for some time: The Afghan government faced an intractable insurgency that would take years to resolve. By that time, both the Taliban and al-Qaeda had regrouped, using bases in the Federally Administered Tribal Area of neighboring Pakistan.

Although the Army had correctly diagnosed the problem by 2008, a change of course would have to wait for the results of that year's presidential election. Addressing cadets at the U.S. Military Academy on December 1, 2009, President Barak Obama announced a new strategy for Afghanistan. He would deploy an additional 30,000 troops to augment the 32,000 already in country. At the same time, he promised that the United States would "begin" to withdraw those troops in 18 months (summer 2011).[135] American forces meanwhile transitioned from a failed counterterrorism strategy to a COIN strategy. "Clear" would be replaced by "clear and hold" as the new guidance for troops on the ground. At the same time, the United States and its NATO allies would improve training for Afghan security forces (army and police), placing greater emphasis on preparing them for COIN operations. The United States also pressured its ally, Pakistan, to be more aggressive in combating the Taliban and al-Qaeda on its side of the border. Furthermore, the United States increased strikes by predator drones against insurgent and terrorist leaders, even targeting these leaders on Pakistani soil. While the government in Islamabad formally condemned the drone attacks, it informally approved them, in some cases even providing the necessary targeting intelligence.

Based on the conclusions of this monograph, the new strategy employs the correct COIN approach, including efforts by the Karzai government to negotiate with the Taliban. However, without the political will to sustain a lengthy campaign, even the best strategy alone will not produce victory. Support for the war in the United States is waning, while it has all but disappeared in Europe, especially since President Obama now speaks of a 2014 end date for the mission with a continued, albeit reduced, presence after that. Despite some recent successes, things have not gone well, concluded a recent CBS News Report:

> The situation in Afghanistan largely deteriorated in 2010, and an endgame—one that involves the United States and its allies departing a stable Afghanistan with a minimal terror threat and the capacity to handle its own security—is as elusive as ever.[136]

A number of factors have contributed to the difficult situation in Afghanistan. First and foremost, the conflict has already degenerated into a chronic insurgency. The Taliban controls large areas of the country and their sphere of control seems to be expanding. While they do use intimidation and terror, their success results in no small measure from their ability to exercise effective shadow governance in the territories they control. The Taliban collects taxes, provides security, and dispenses justice. In 2008, they ran 13 "guerrilla courts," hearing civil and criminal cases based on their version of shari'a law, often with greater fairness (at least in the eyes of local Pashtuns) than the official courts.[137] The Taliban funds their activity by taxing all phases of opium production from poppy cultivation to refinement through smuggling.[138] As long as this situation persists, the insurgents do not have to win an outright victory. They can pursue an "exhaustion strategy," wearing down ISAF until it withdraws and the Karzai government collapses.[139] This strategy shows every sign of working. At the November 2010 NATO summit, troop contributors reluctantly agreed to extend their deployment to 2014 and to maintain a training mission beyond that date. In a deliberately vague statement, NATO Secretary- General Fogh Rasmussen stated that he did not "foresee (allied) troops in a combat role beyond 2014, provided, of course, that the security situation allows us to move into a more supportive role."[140] President Karzai also wants foreign troops out of his country and supports the 2014 withdrawal date.

Afghanistan's neighbors further compound its security problems. Iran, one of the most implacable of U.S. enemies, allows aid to flow across its border to the insurgents. Pakistan, however, presents the greatest challenge. The Pashtun community to which the insurgents belong extends across the ill-defined and almost completely porous border between the two countries. The Pakistani government exercises little meaningful sovereignty over the Federally Administered Tribal Area along its northwest frontier, a buffer zone created to protect British India, out of which the Taliban and al-Qaeda operate. Islamabad plays a double game, publically backing the United States, while privately aiding the Taliban whom it understandably believes may yet win the war. Objectionable as such duplicity may be, it makes sense given Pakistan's geopolitical situation. The United States and its allies will leave sooner or later, while Afghanistan will remain indefinitely as a neighbor and a security concern. Before the U.S.-led occupation, Islamabad had backed the Taliban as part of its defense-in-depth strategy against India, reasoning that a radical Islamist government in Kabul would have nothing to do with New Delhi. Only under extreme pressure did it reluctantly agree to support the United States, a decision which remains widely unpopular among the Pakistani people.

These disadvantages notwithstanding, the United States can still get an acceptable outcome from the Afghanistan mission, provided it understands that "acceptable" does not mean "ideal." Resolving Afghanistan's chronic insurgency requires replacing Taliban shadow governance with legitimate state sovereignty. The complexity of the situation, the number of state, non-state, and quasi-state actors precludes any simple solution to this problem. Any successful strategy will take several years to implement and longer to bear fruit. Such a strategy might seek complete victory, but all available evidence suggests that the conflict will be more easily resolved through negotiation and compromise, just like the Group 4 cases discussed herein.

The Afghan government, supported by the United States and ISAF, might continue its no-compromise-with-terrorists-or-insurgents policy. This approach would require maintaining ISAF troop strength at least at current levels and spending billions of dollars in aid over at least the next decade. Such aid would have to be delivered according to a unified plan that strengthened rather than weakened Afghan sovereignty. For its part, the Karzai government would have to eliminate or at least seriously reduce corruption and commit to truly democratic reform. These measures would probably not succeed, however, unless the government of Pakistan committed to a determined, sustained effort to eradicate Taliban and al-Qaeda safe havens on its side of the border. Given the sympathy for the Taliban within Pakistan's Inter-Services Intelligence Department and even the Pakistani army, the fragile nature of the Pakistani state and the growing anti-Americanism among the Pakistani population, such whole-hearted cooperation seems unlikely. Asking the Karzai administration to clamp down on corruption engaged in by the President's own family seems an equally tall order. Meanwhile, U.S. public support for the sustained effort necessary to defeat the Taliban also seems to be waning. Thus while an all-out-victory strategy would produce the most desirable result, it is also the most costly and the least likely to succeed.

As an alternative, the Afghan government, supported by the United States and its allies, could adopt a strategy of co-option, inviting the Taliban into a power-sharing agreement. Power sharing might involve dividing up government offices and/or some sort of federalized division of the country. This approach presupposes willingness on the part of the Taliban to negotiate such an arrangement. However, the experience of Northern Ireland suggests that power sharing only becomes possible when both sides reach a military stalemate and see no value in continuing the armed struggle. Given its revival and expansion into Pakistan over the past 4 years, the Taliban has every reason to believe that it is winning. At this point, it has little to gain from compromise. In addition, the Taliban leadership seems to have absorbed al-Qaeda's mission of continuing jihad, making them very unwilling to negotiate with infidels and heretics. Whether these sentiments are genuine or merely rhetoric to help them gain outside support in the struggle for power in Afghanistan remains to be seen.

As a third option (a variation of the co-option strategy), the Afghan government, backed by the U.S.-led coalition, might fight the Taliban to a stalemate and then reach an accommodation with it, recognizing Taliban control of some Afghan territory. Such an accommodation might be the basis for a ceasefire and negotiations. It also might result in a de facto partition of Afghanistan and might encourage the Taliban to create "Pashtunistan" by uniting with Pashtun tribes in Pakistan. Creating a Pashtun state (de facto or de jure) could, however, cause Pakistan to implode and become the world's first nuclear failed state.

A fourth option would be to divide and rule, not from the top down, but from the bottom up. This approach would require exploiting the same cleavages within tribal society that the Taliban have used so successfully against the Afghan government. David Kilcullen estimates that 90 percent of Taliban supporters within Afghanistan are "actually or potentially co-optable," though he insists that co-option would have to be done from a position of strength.[141] For such a strategy to work, the Karzai administration would have to engage in meaningful reform to eliminate corruption and re-incorporate disaffected tribal leaders into local power structures, perhaps removing some of his patronage appointees. It would also require reversing the shift of power promoted by the Taliban from Maliks (tribal leaders) back to Mullahs (religious leaders) in local communities and fostering sustainable grassroots development projects to improve the quality of Afghan life. Finally, the poppy eradication effort would need to be brought into harmony with the COIN campaign instead of being implemented in its current haphazard, often unfair, manner, which hurts small farmers while leaving large drug traffickers untouched.[142] None of these measures will be possible without security, which means more ISAF and Afghan troops to engage the Taliban and protect local communities. At the same time, the government of Pakistan must eliminate or at least reduce Taliban sanctuaries in its country. This approach offers the best chance of success, but it is a tall order to fill and will require a sustained commitment from the United States and its allies for several years.

The United States is pursuing this sort of bottom-up strategy while leaving open the door to a negotiated settlement. "You really have to take it a district at a time—and maybe even more local areas than that," Secretary of Defense Robert Gates told National Public Radio in December 2010, "and diversify your strategy depending on the local conditions, in terms of whether presence contributes to security or detracts from security. And that may differ from one valley to the next."[143] At the same time that it employs this grassroots strategy, the U.S.-led coalition continues to pressure the Karzai government to diminish corruption and the Pakistani government to move more aggressively against Taliban safe havens on its territory, especially those in North Waziristan. Meanwhile, training of Afghan security forces continues. While the current strategy contains the right combination of activities, time seems to be working against it. "We are breaking the momentum of the enemy and will eventually reverse it," Gates added during a December 2010 trip to Afghanistan. "It will be a while, and we will suffer tougher losses as we go."[144] However, "a while" may be more time than the United States has. Canada will withdraw its troops in July 2011, and British Prime Minister David Cameron hinted during his December 2010 visit to Afghanistan that he might begin to bring British troops home at about the same time, well ahead of the 2014 withdrawal date already announced.[145] Loss of these two NATO allies, the ones whose troops have been most willing to fight the Taliban, would be a serious blow to the U.S.-led coalition.

Richard Haass, a member of the Bush administration foreign policy team, proposes a different version of the grassroots strategy. Arguing that nothing the United States is likely to achieve is worth the $100 billion a year being spent on Afghanistan and the increasing number of U.S. lives being lost in the conflict, he proposes paying less attention to the Afghan government and supporting local leaders instead. This "decentralization" strategy would, he maintains, restore the historic political balance in a country long characterized by local autonomy and weak central government. Instead of partition, this approach might produce a "patchwork" quilt.[146] However, as the UN plans for Palestine (1947) and Bosnia (1993) have shown, political quilts do not work very well in ethnically divided war zones.

There is, of course, a distinct possibility that the conflict cannot be brought to a satisfactory conclusion at an acceptable cost in blood and treasure no matter what strategy the United States employs. The White House and Pentagon should develop a worse-case exit strategy, but even such an undesirable scenario will require U.S. engagement with Afghanistan and its neighbors. Some conflicts need to be contained and managed rather than won. If the Taliban does return to power and refuses to reach an accommodation with Washington, the United States might revive the old Northern Alliance as a foil for Kabul, although this would probably result in de facto partition of the country. The United States might also make clear that it would hold any government in Kabul accountable for terrorist attacks launched from Afghan soil, threatening to strike the country with stand-off weapons in retaliation, a tactic that would put no U.S. service personnel at risk.

CONCLUSION

For almost 30 years following the Vietnam War, the U.S. Army and many academics considered COIN part of a receding colonial past, unlikely to trouble them in the foreseeable future. Two protracted internal wars have disabused everyone of that illusion. Insurgency and counterinsurgency are here to stay. While no one in the U.S. military any longer doubts this fact, how best to prepare for future COIN conflicts remains problematic. The American military must maintain its readiness to fight a conventional war anywhere in the world while continuing to develop its unconventional capability, struggling to educate and train that critical commodity, the two-speed soldier — an effective war fighter who can also meet the challenges of COIN. As it meets this challenge, the United States must look to its own experience and to that of other nations. The road to the future lies through the past, via a careful analysis not of a narrow selection of colonial COIN campaigns, but through consideration of a broader selection of cases such as those presented in this monograph.

ENDNOTES

1. Mark T. Burger and Douglas A. Border, "The Long War: Insurgency, Counterinsurgency and Collapsing States," *Third World Quarterly*, Vol. 28, No. 2, 2007, p. 199.

2. *U.S. Government Counterinsurgency Guide*, Washington, DC: Department of State, 2009, p. 17.

3. William Rosenau, "Subversion and Terrorism: Understanding and Countering the Threat," *The MIPT Terrorism Annual, 2006*, Oklahoma City, OK: MIPT, 2006, p. 53.

4. David Kilcullen, "Counterinsurgency *Redux*," *Survival*, Vol. 48, No. 4, December 1, 2006, p. 1.

5. Ben Connable and Martin C. Libicki, *How Insurgencies End*, Santa Monica, CA: Rand, 2010.

6. Christopher Paul, Colin P. Clarke, and Beth Grill, *Victory has a Thousand Fathers*, Santa Monica, CA: Rand, 2010.

7. This monograph grew out of my paper, "How Insurgencies End," presented to the Rand Insurgency Board in March 2008.

8. *DOD Dictionary of Military and Associated Terms*, available from *www.dtic.mil/doctrine/dod_dictionary/*.

9. Thomas R. Mockaitis, *British Counterinsurgency: 1919-1960*, London, UK: Macmillan, 1990, p. 3.

10. Rosenau, pp. 55-58.

11. *U.S. Government Counterinsurgency Guide*, p. 6.

12. *Convention (II) with Respect to the Laws and Customs of War on Land and its Annex: Regulations Concerning the Laws and Customs of War on Land*, The Hague, July 29, 1899, Annex I, Chap. 1, Sec. 1, Art. 1, translated and available on the International Committee of the Red Cross website, *www.icrc.org/ihl.nsf/FULL/150?OpenDocument*.

13. Nils Melzer, *Interpretive Guidance on the Notion of Direct Participation in Hostilities under Humanitarian Law*, Geneva, Switzerland: International Committee of the Red Cross (ICRC), 2009, p. 20.

14. William Boothby, "Direct Participation in Hostilities: Perspectives on the ICRC Interpretive Guidance: 'And for Such Time As': The Time Dimension to Direct Participation in Hostilities," *New York University Journal of Law and Politics*, No. 741, Spring 2010, online edition, available from *www.lexisnexis.com.ezproxy1. lib.depaul.edu/hottopics/lnacademic/*.

15. George Rudé, *Revolutionary Europe, 1783-1815*, New York: Harper, 1964, p. 74.

16. For a discussion of organizational structure, see Christopher Harmon, *Terrorism Today*, London, UK: Frank Cass, 2000, pp. 96-101.

17. For a discussion of terror and those who use it, see Thomas R. Mockaitis, *The "New" Terrorism: Myths and Reality*, Westport, CT: Praeger, 2007, pp. 2-9.

18. Thomas P. Thornton, "Terror as a Weapon of Political Agitation," Harry Eckstein, ed., *Internal War: Problems and Approaches,* New York: The Free Press, 1964, pp. 72-73.

19. Robert Cribb, "Introduction," Eric Wilson, ed., *Government of the Shadows: Parapolitics and Criminal Sovereignty*, New York: Pluto Press, 2009, p. 1.

20. For British approach to COIN on which this discussion is based, see Thomas Mockaitis, *British Counterinsurgency* and *British Counterinsurgency in the Post-Imperial Era,* Manchester, UK: Manchester U. Press, 1995.

21. Bernard B. Fall, quoted in David Kilcullen, *The Accidental Guerrilla: Fighting Small Wars in the Midst of a Big One,* New York: Oxford, 2009, p. 88.

22. Jackie Northan, "As Afghan Conflict Escalates, What Went Wrong?," "All Things Considered," National Public Radio, De-

cember 9, 2010, available from *www.npr.org/2010/12/09/131940690/ As-Afghan-Conflict-Escalates-What-Went-Wrong.*

23. Michael R. Turner and General Bernard M. Trainor, *Cobra II: The Inside Story of the Invasion and Occupation of Iraq*, New York: Vintage Books, 2006.

24. A. H. Maslow, "A Theory of Human Motivation," *Psychological Review*, Vol. 50, No. 4, 1943, pp. 370-396.

25. David Kilcullen, "Road Building in Afghanistan," *Small Wars Journal*, online edition, April 24, 2008, available from *smallwarsjournal.com/blog/2008/04/political-maneuver-in-counteri/.*

26. Frank Kitson, *Bunch of Five*, London, UK: Faber and Faber, 1977, p. 298.

27. *Field Manual (FM) 3-24: Counterinsurgency*, Washington, DC: Department of the Army, 2006, pp. 1-26.

28. *National Military Strategy for the War on Terrorism*, Washington, DC: Chairman, Joint Chiefs of Staff, 2006, p. 13.

29. See Robert Taber, *The War of the Flea: A Study of Guerrilla Warfare Theory and Practice*, New York: Potomac Books, 2002; 1st Ed., 1965.

30. J. Bowyer Bell, *The Myth of the Guerrilla: Revolutionary Theory and Malpractice*, New York: Knopf, 1971, challenges Taber's argument.

31. McMahon-Hussein Correspondence, July 14, 1915, to March 10, 1916, available from Middle East Website, *www.mideastweb.org/mcmahon.htm.*

32. Letter of Arthur James Balfour to Lord Rothschild, *Sunday Times*, UK, November 9, 1917, available from TIMESARCHIVE, *archive.timesonline.co.uk/tol/viewArticle.arc?articleId=ARCHIVE-The_Times-1917-11-09-07-010&pageId=ARCHIVE-The_ Times-1917-11-09-07.*

33. Sykes-Picot Agreement, May 15-16, 1916, available from WWI Document Archive, *wwi.lib.byu.edu/index.php/Sykes-Picot_Agreement.*

34. 1939 (MacDonald) White Paper, available from *avalon.law. yale.edu/20th_century/brwh1939.asp.*

35. John Marlowe, *The Seat of Pilate,* London, UK: 1959, pp. 171-172. Haganah leader and later Israeli Defense Minister Moshe Dayan insists that they received only shotguns from the British and smuggled in better weapons. *Moshe Dayan: Story of My Life, An Autobiography,* New York: Sphere Books, 1976, p. 33.

36. David Charters, *The British Army and the Jewish Insurgency in Palestine,* London, UK: Macmillan, 1989, p. 41.

37. *Ibid.,* pp. 43, 46, 48.

38. For analysis of the British response, see Mockaitis, *British Counterinsurgency,* pp. 101-111.

39. General Miles Dempsey to the War Office, November 16, 1946, Imperial War Museum, Bernard Law Montgomery Papers, BLM/211/2.

40. Lieutenant Colonel Philippe Francois, "Waging Counterinsurgency in Algeria: A French Perspective," *Military Review,* September-October 2008, p. 59.

41. *Ibid.,* p. 60.

42. Colonel Giles Martin, "War in Algeria: the French Experience," *Military Review,* July-August 2005, p. 53.

43. *Ibid.*

44. Keith Sutton, "Administration Tensions over Algeria's Centres de Regroupment, 1954-1962," *British Journal of Middle East Studies,* Vol. 26, No. 2, November 1999, pp. 243-270.

45. Francois, pp. 66-67.

46. UNHCR *et al.*, *Kosovo Atlas*, Pristina, Kosovo: UNHCR, 2000, p. vi.

47. Howard Clark, *Civil Resistance in Kosovo*, London, UK: Pluto Press, 2000, pp. 95-121.

48. Miron Rezun, *Europe's Nightmare: The Struggle for Kosovo*, Westport, CT: Praeger, 2001, pp. 40, 45-46.

49. Ivo Daalder and Michael O'Hanlon, *Winning Ugly: NATO's War to Save Kosovo*, Washington, DC: The Brookings Institution, 2000, p. 27.

50. Rezun, p. 44.

51. This argument is the premise of Bowyer Bell, *Myth of the Guerrilla.*

52. R. W. Komer, *The Malayan Emergency in Retrospect: Organization of a Successful Counterinsurgency Effort*, Santa Monica, CA: Rand, 1972, pp. 2-3.

53. For a detailed discussion of the British approach to COIN, see Mockaitis, *British Counterinsurgency, 1919-1960.*

54. For a discussion of the Briggs Plan, see *ibid.*, pp. 115-116.

55. Anthony Short, *The Communist Insurrection in Malay, 1948-1960*, London, UK: Muller, 1975, p. 403.

56. "Director of Operations, Malaya Directive No. 13: Administration of Chinese Settlement," February 26, 1951, PRO, CO 1022/132.

57. David Lloyd Owen, Assistant to Gerald Templer, to Lewis J. Hankings, April 15, 1969, National Army Museum, UK, Accession No. 8011-132.

58. FM 3-24, pp. 1-26.

59. Quoted in Robert Thompson, *Defeating Communist Insurgency: the Lessons of Malaya and Vietnam*, London, UK: Chatto and Windus, 1966, p. 61.

60. Michael McClintock, *Instruments of Statecraft: U.S. Guerrilla Warfare, COIN, and Counter-Terrorism, 1940-1990*, New York: Pantheon Books, 1992, p. 12.

61. Andrew J. Birtle, *U.S. Army COIN and Contingency Operations Doctrine, 1942-1976*, Washington, DC: U.S. Army Center for Military History, 2006, p. 47-48.

62. *Ibid.*, p. 52.

63. Preeti Bhattacharji, "Liberation Tigers of Tamil Eelam, aka Tamil Tigers, Sri Lanka, separatists, " Council on Foreign Relations "Backgrounder," updated May 20, 2009, available from *www.cfr.org/publication/9242/liberation_tigers_of_tamil_eelam_aka_tamil_tigers_sri_lanka_separatists.html*.

64. Jayshree Bajoria, "The Sri Lankan Conflict," Council on Foreign Affairs, "Backgrounder," updated May 18, 2009, available from *www.cfr.org/publication/11407/sri_lankan_conflict.html#*.

65. For discussion of Tamil governance, see Kristian Stokke, "Building the Tamil Eelam State: Emerging State Institutions and Forms of Governance in LTTE-Controlled Areas in Sri Lanka," *Third World Quarterly*, Vol. 27, No. 6, 2006, pp. 1021-1040.

66. Details on LTTE fundraising from K. Alan Kronstadt and Bruce Vaughn, *Sri Lanka: Background and U.S. Relations*, Washington, DC: Congressional Research Service, June 4, 2009, p. 10.

67. *Ibid.*

68. *Ibid.*

69. Bhattacharji.

70. Andrew Hosken, Interview with Colonel Karuna Amman, BBC Today, May 5, 2009, available from *news.bbc.co.uk/today/hi/today/newsid_8033000/8033150.stm*.

71. "Who are ETA?" BBC Online, November 17, 2008, available from *news.bbc.co.uk/2/hi/europe/3500728.stm*.

72. Available from *www.fas.org/irp/world/para/eta.htm*.

73. Jan Oskar Engene, *Terrorism in Western Europe: Explaining the Trends since 1980,* North Hampton, MA: Edward Elgar, 2004, p. 133.

74. ETA killed 474 people between 1967 and 1995. *Ibid.*, p. 129.

75. *Ibid.*, p. 130.

76. *Ibid.*

77. Lewis Taylor, "Counter-Insurgency Strategy, the PCP-Sendero Luminoso and the Civil War in Peru, 1980-1996," *Bulletin of Latin American Research*, Vol. 17, No. 1, January 1998, p. 41.

78. Kathryn Gregory, "Shining Path, Túpac Amaru, (Peru, leftists)," Council on Foreign Relations, August 27, 2009, available from *www.cfr.org/publication/9276/shining_path_tupac_amaru_peru_leftists.html*.

79. *Ibid.*, p. 41.

80. Angela Cornell and Kenneth Roberts, "Democracy, Counterinsurgency, and Human Rights: The Case of Peru," *Human Rights Quarterly*, Vol. 12, No. 4, November 1990, p. 536.

81. *Ibid.*, p. 540.

82. Robert B. Kent, "Geographical Dimensions of Shining Path Insurgency in Peru," *Geographical Review*, Vol. 83, No. 4, October 1993, p. 449.

83. *Ibid.*, p. 541.

84. *Ibid.*, p. 449.

85. For a discussion of British influence on the Peruvian COIN campaign, see Taylor, "Counter-Insurgency Strategy, the PCP-Sendero Luminoso and the Civil War in Peru."

86. *Ibid.*, p. 51.

87. *Ibid.*

88. James Zackrison, "Colombia," Yonah Alexander, ed., *Combating Terrorism: Strategies of Ten Countries,* Ann Arbor: University of Michigan Press, 2002, p. 118.

89. *Ibid.*

90. *Ending Colombia's FARC Conflict: Dealing the Right Card,* Washington, DC: International Crisis Group, 2009, p. 4.

91. See, for example, Stephen Flynn, *U.S. Support of Plan Colombia: Rethinking the Ends and Means,* Carlisle, PA: Strategic Studies Institute, U.S. Army War College, 2002.

92. Luis Nagle, *Plan Colombia: Reality of the Colombian Crisis and Implications for Hemispheric Security,* Carlisle, PA: Strategic Studies Institute, U.S. Army War College, 2002, p. 8.

93. *Ibid.*, p. 9.

94. *Ibid.*, p. 7.

95. *Ending Colombia's FARC Conflict,* p. 5.

96. *Ibid.*, p. 7.

97. *Ibid.*

98. "Improving Security Policy in Colombia," Policy Briefing, Bogotá: International Crisis Group, 2010, pp. 3-6.

99. Flynn, p. 5.

100. *War and Drugs in Colombia,* International Crisis Group: 2005, p. 10.

101. *Ibid.*, p. 11.

102. Tom Wilson, *Ulster: Conflict and Consent,* London, UK: Basil Blackwell, 1989, p. 107.

103. Michael Dewar, *The British Army in Northern Ireland,* London, UK: Arms and Armour Press, 1985, p. 47.

104. *Ibid.*

105. "Building on Success: the Story of Northern Ireland Housing since 1970," Background Brief, London, UK: Foreign and Commonwealth Office, 1992, p. 1.

106. This is the premise of the article by J. Bowyer Bell, "An Irish War: The IRA's Armed Struggle, 1969-1980, Strategy as History Rules OK," *Small Wars and Insurgencies,* Vol. 1, No. 3, December 1990.

107. Richard English, *Armed Struggle: The History of the IRA,* New York: Oxford, 2003, p. 315.

108. Benjamin Schwartz, *American Counterinsurgency Doctrine and El Salvador: the Frustrations of Reform and the Illusions of National Building,* Santa Monica, CA: Rand Corporation, 1991, p. 9.

109. *Ibid.,* p. 103.

110. William Dean Stanley, "State Building Before and After Democratization: 1980-1995," Vol. 27, No. 1, 2006, p. 102.

111. *Ibid.*

112. Schwartz, p. 103.

113. Charles T. Call, "War and State-Building: Constructing the Rule of Law in El Salvador," *Journal of Latin American Studies,* Vol. 35, No. 4, November, 2003, p. 831.

114. Ricardo Córdova Macías, "Demilitarizing and Democratizing Salvadoran Politics," Margarita S. Studemeister, *El Salvador Implementation of the Peace Accords,* Washington, DC: U.S. Institute of Peace, 2001, p. 128.

115. Call, p. 831.

116. Demographic details from *World Fact Book*, Washington, DC: Central Intelligence Agency, 1991, pp. 1089, 1092.

117. Anyu D. Ndumbe, "Diamonds, Ethnicity, and Power: the Case of Sierra Leone," *Mediterranean Quarterly*, Vol. 12, No. 4, Fall 2001, p. 94.

118. *Ibid.*, p. 99.

119. Text of Lomé Accords, available from *www.sierra-leone. org/lomeaccord.html*.

120. "Seventeenth Report of the Secretary-General on the United Nations Mission in Sierra Leone," UN Document S/2003/321, March 17, 2003.

121. "Twenty-Seventh Report of the Secretary-General on the United Nations Mission in Sierra Leone," UN Document S/2005/777, December 12, 2005.

122. "Review of the Outcome of the High-level Special Session of the Peacebuilding Commission on Sierra Leon," PBC4/SLE/3, October 10, 2010.

123. Richard N. Haass, "We're Not Winning. It's Not Worth It," *Newsweek*, July 18, 2010, online edition, available from *www.newsweek.com/2010/07/18/we-re-not-winning-it-s-not-worth-it.html*.

124. Colonel (Ret.) Timothy Heinemann, "Memorandum for US SOCOM Historian," observations on his role in Operation IRAQI FREEDOM, September 14, 2004.

125. *Field Manual (FM) 100-20: Military Operations in Low-Intensity Conflict*, Washington, DC: Department of the Army, 1990, p. 2-15.

126. Paul, Clarke, and Grill, *Victory has a Thousand Fathers*, p. 97.

127. Thomas R. Mockaitis, "Counterinsurgency Doctrine: the U.S. Experience," Jan Angstrom and Isabelle Duyvesteyn, *Modern War and the Utility of Force: Challenges, Methods, and Strategy*, London, UK: Routledge, 2010, pp. 142-158.

128. FM 100-20, p. 2-15.

129. *Joint Publication (JP) 3-07: Doctrine for Joint Operations in Low-Intensity Conflict*, Washington, DC: The Joint Staff, 1994, p. II-5.

130. Burger and Border, "The Long War: Insurgency, Counterinsurgency and Collapsing States," p. 198.

131. James A. Baker III and Lee Hamilton *et al.*, *Report of the Iraq Study Group*, Washington, DC: U.S. Institute of Peace, 2006, p. 6.

132. Details on the origin and growth of the "Anbar Awakening" from Alissa J. Rueben and Damien Cave, "In a Force for Iraqi Calm, Seeds of Conflict," *The New York Times*, online edition, December 23, 2007, available from *www.nytimes.com/2007/12/23/world/middleeast/23awakening.html?_r=1&pagewanted=all*.

133. Thomas R. Mockaitis, *Iraq and the Challenge of Counterinsurgency*, Westport, CT: Praeger, 2008, p. 143.

134. Ahmed Rashid, *Descent into Chaos: The United States and the Failure of Nation Building in Pakistan, Afghanistan, and Central Asia*, New York: Penguin, 2008, p. 21.

135. Transcript of President Barak Obama's Speech Delivered at West Point, December 1, 2010, available from *abcnews.go.com/Politics/full-transcript-president-obamas-speech-afghanistan-delivered-west-point/story?id=9220661*.

136. Brian Montopoli, "In Afghanistan War, No Clear End in Sight," CBS News Online, November 15, 2010, available from *www.cbsnews.com/8301-503544_162-20022855-503544.html?tag=cbsnewsMainColumnArea*.

137. David Kilcullen, *The Accidental Guerrilla: Fighting Small Wars in the Midst of a Big One*, New York: Oxford, 2009, p. 76.

138. For a discussion of the opium trade, militias, and Taliban funding, see Gretchen S. Peters, "The Taliban and the Opium Trade," Antonio Giustozzi, ed., *Decoding the Taliban: Insights from the Afghan Field*, London, UK: Hurst, 2009, pp. 6-22.

139. Kilcullen, *The Accidental Guerrilla*, p. 81.

140. Christi Parsons and Paul Richter, "NATO Hedges Afghan Pullout," *Chicago Tribune*, November 21, 2010, Sec. 1, p. 31.

141. Kilcullen, *The Accidental Guerrilla*, p. 78.

142. *Ibid.*, p. 94.

143. Quoted in Rachel Martin, "Gates Visits Afghanistan Ahead of War Review," December 7, 2010, National Public Radio online, available from *www.npr.org/2010/12/07/131882442/gates-visits-afghanistan-ahead-of-war-review*.

144. The Associated Press, "Gates Sees Hard-Won Success in East Afghanistan," National Public Radio online, available from *www.npr.org/templates/story/story.php?storyId=131868579*.

145. "Wikileaks 'will not damage UK-Afghan relations'," BBC online, December 7, 2010, available from *www.bbc.co.uk/news/uk-politics-11933476?cid=dlvr.it*.

146. Haass.

www.ingramcontent.com/pod-product-compliance
Lightning Source LLC
Chambersburg PA
CBHW072331290526
45794CB00002B/834